Robert Frank
Trolley—New Orleans

LUCY GALLUN

THE MUSEUM OF MODERN ART, NEW YORK

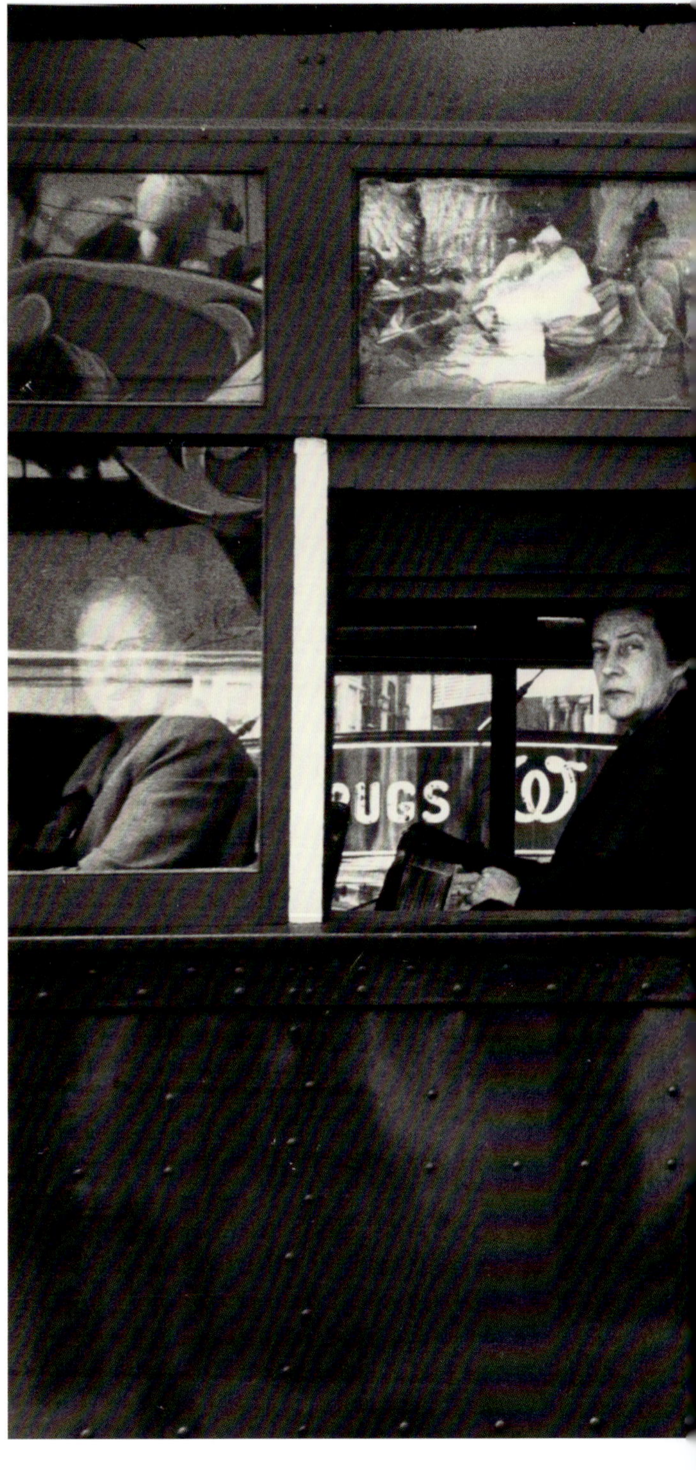

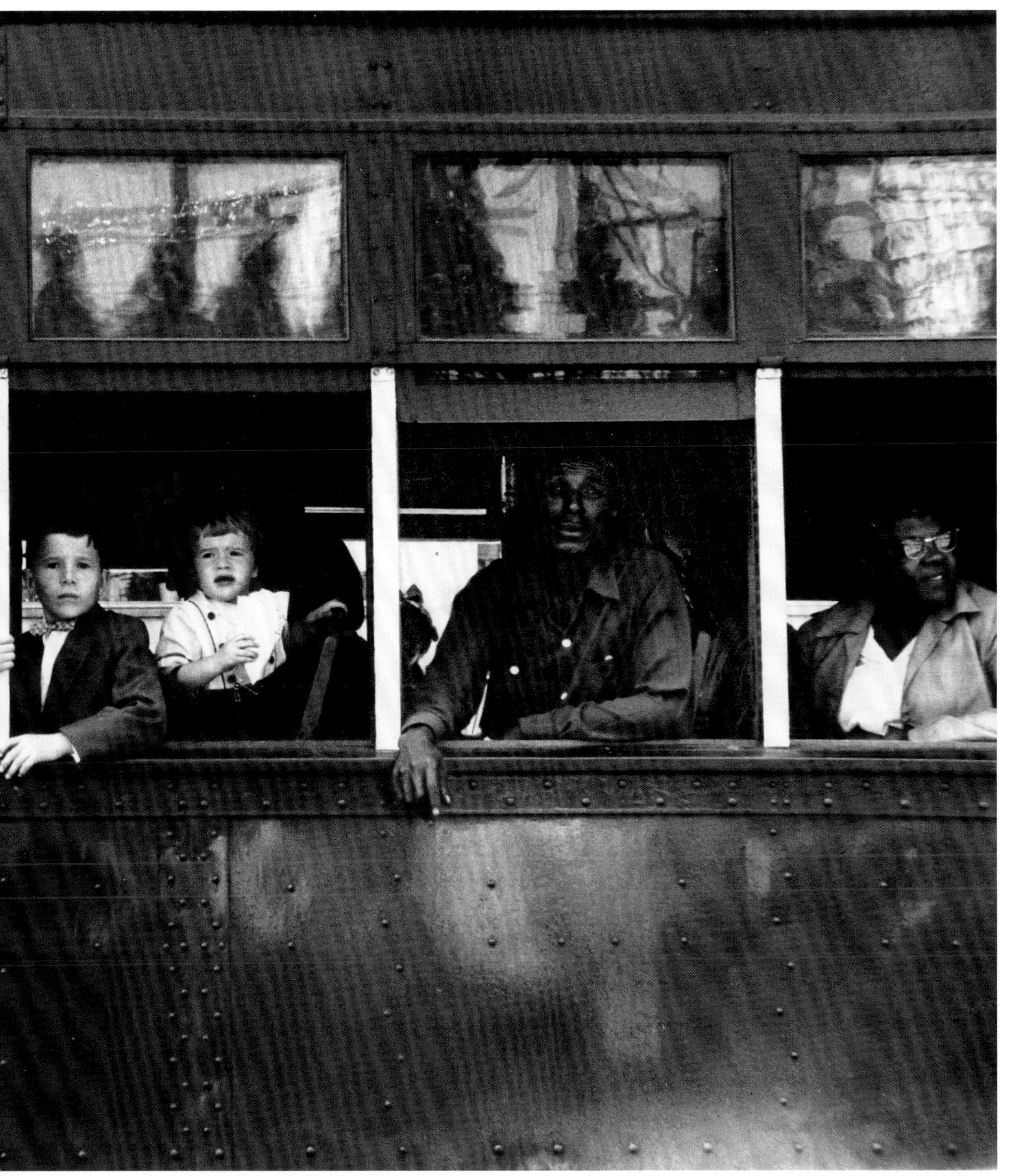

Robert Frank (American, born Switzerland. 1924–2019). *Trolley—New Orleans*. 1955. Gelatin silver print, 9 1/16 × 13 3/8" (23.1 × 34 cm). THE MUSEUM OF MODERN ART, NEW YORK. THE FELLOWS OF PHOTOGRAPHY FUND, THE FAMILY OF MAN FUND, AND HORACE W. GOLDSMITH FUND THROUGH ROBERT B. MENSCHEL

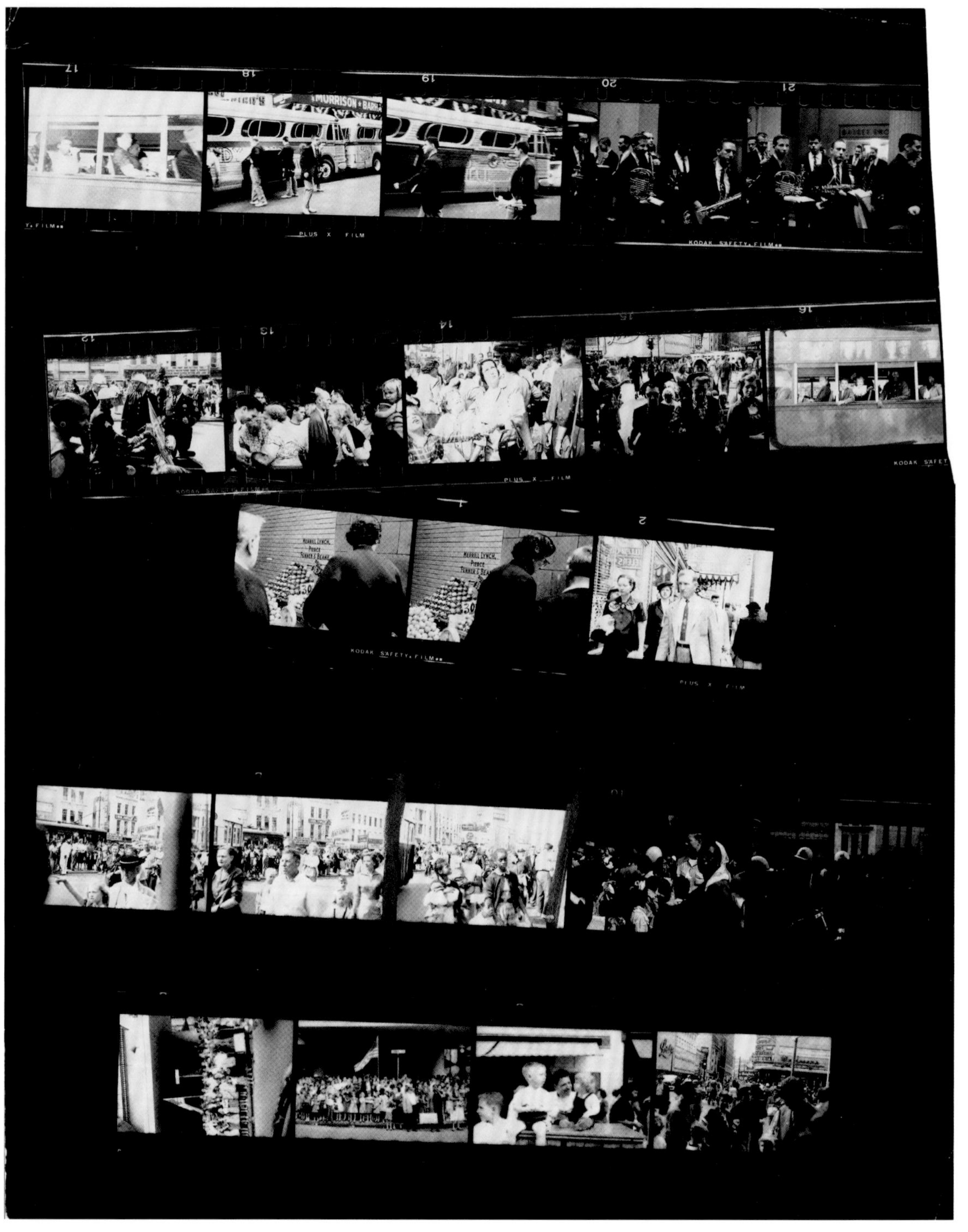

FIG. 1. Robert Frank (American, born Switzerland. 1924–2019). Contact sheet from the portfolio *Robert Frank: The Americans, 81 Contact Sheets*. November 11, 1955. Inkjet print, printed 2009, 20 ¼ × 16 $\frac{9}{16}$" (51.5 × 42 cm). THE MUSEUM OF MODERN ART, NEW YORK. GIFT OF SUSAN AND PETER MACGILL

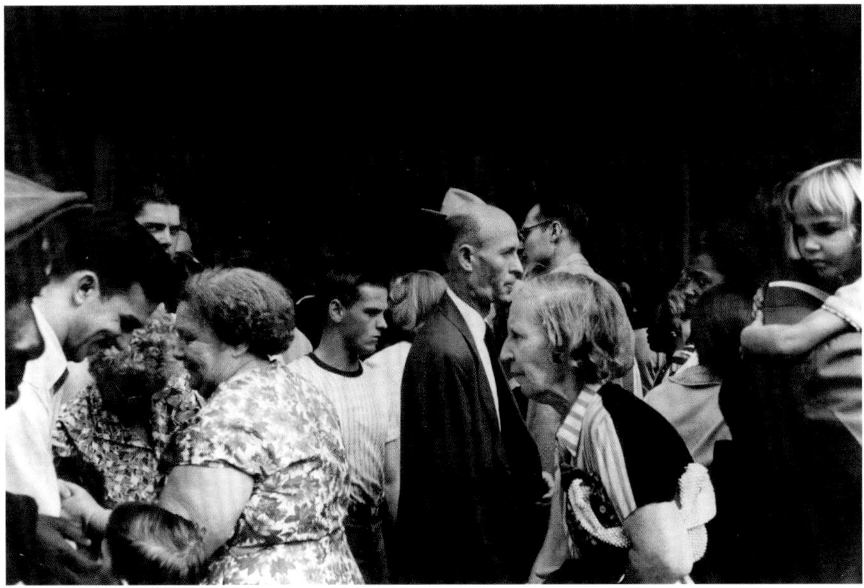

FIG. 2. Robert Frank (American, born Switzerland. 1924–2019). *Canal Street—New Orleans*. 1955. Gelatin silver print, 8 ¼ × 12 5⁄16" (20.9 × 31.3 cm). THE MUSEUM OF MODERN ART, NEW YORK. GIFT OF ROBERT AND GAYLE GREENHILL

"AMERICA IS AN INTERESTING COUNTRY, BUT THERE IS A LOT HERE THAT I DO not like and that I would never accept," the Swiss-born photographer Robert Frank wrote in a letter to his parents in late 1955. "I am also trying to show this in my photos."[1] On November 11 of that year, Frank was passing through New Orleans on the multi-leg road trip that would produce his landmark book *The Americans*. Turning away from the throngs of people crowding Canal Street, he pointed his camera at a streetcar and clicked the shutter, creating the image he would later title *Trolley—New Orleans*. Frank's contact sheet from this roll of film shows that the sidewalks around him were teeming with people of all ages: young musicians in matching blazers; grinning police officers gathered around their motorcycles; elderly women with arms linked **[FIG. 1]**. Three frames before the streetcar, he captured a section of Canal Street jam-packed with pedestrians crossing within inches of one another, intent on their own business **[FIG. 2]**.[2] In *Trolley*, on the other hand, Frank isolated the faces of just a few individuals, as they sat, immobile, framed by the vehicle's windows.

The order of the passengers in the streetcar mirrors the unjust social order of the world around them: The figure at left, seated nearest to the front of the vehicle, appears to be a white man, partially obscured by reflections in the glass between him and the camera. In the row behind him is a white woman, her lips

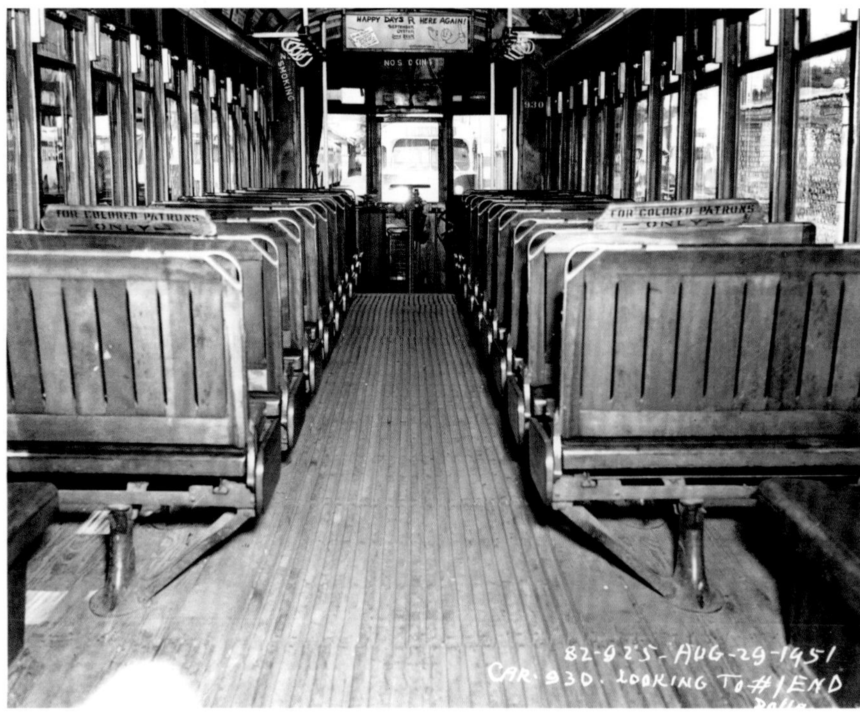

FIG. 3. Interior of a streetcar with race screens, New Orleans, August 29, 1951. CHARLES L. FRANCK STUDIO COLLECTION AT THE HISTORIC NEW ORLEANS COLLECTION

clenched, almost scowling as she looks directly out at the photographer through the open window. At far right, in the rearmost row visible within the frame of the photograph, a Black woman gazes away from the camera. In front of her a Black man in a work shirt leans on the window frame, his hand hanging heavy over the edge; he, too, seems to meet the photographer's eye. In the middle, two white children share a bench—a boy, sharply dressed in a bowtie, staring straight at the camera, and a younger girl behind him. One of her hands grips a white paper bag; the other rests on the little wooden sign, known as a race screen, that divides the front of the streetcar, reserved for white passengers, from the rear, and which could be picked up and moved back by the white passengers to assure themselves of a seat as the vehicle filled **[FIG. 3]**.

"I had always tried to come up with a picture that really said it all, that was a masterpiece," Frank once reflected, but by "the time I applied for the Guggenheim Fellowship by the middle '50s, I decided that wasn't it either. . . . I decided that there had to be a more sustained form of visual expression. There had to be more pictures that would sustain an idea or vision or something. I couldn't just depend on that one singular photograph anymore."[3] Indeed, the monumental

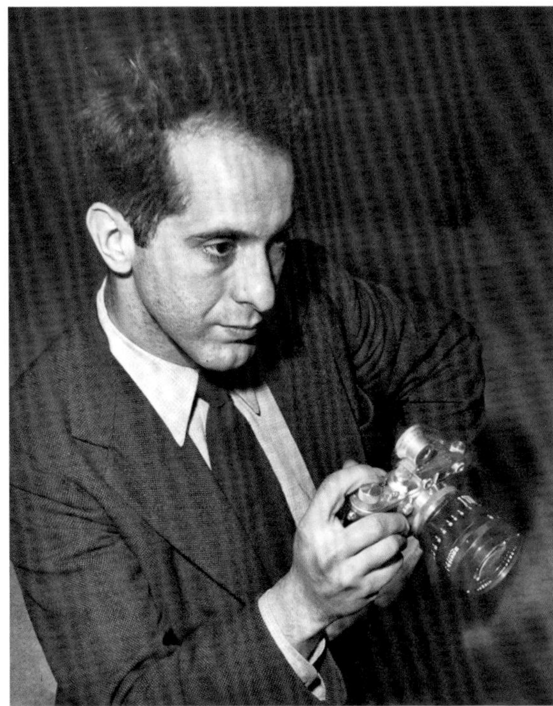

FIG. 4. Fred Stein (American, 1909–1967). *Robert Frank*. 1954. Gelatin silver print, 9 7/8 x 7 15/16" (25.1 x 20.1 cm). THE MUSEUM OF MODERN ART ARCHIVES, NEW YORK

work that came out of Frank's 1955 Guggenheim Fellowship—*The Americans*—is just that: a sustained idea woven from eighty-three photographs shot over two years in urban and rural environments in multiple states, a carefully sequenced rhythm of images creating a layered and complex portrait of the United States and the people who lived there. Nonetheless, *Trolley*, the photograph that appeared on the cover of the U.S. edition of the book, is a singular work of art, a picture that has transcended its original context through its reverberating influences, even as it distills many of the characteristics of *The Americans*. Its impacts are at once political, social, and artistic. It is, in the words of Frank's fellow photographer and one-time collaborator Danny Lyon, "a perfect picture."[4]

In his Guggenheim Fellowship application, Frank anticipated that his work would be read through the lens of social documentary—as a cultural portrait of the United States—but he emphasized his own aesthetic aims as well: "It is only partly documentary in nature: one of its aims is more artistic than the word documentary implies."[5] One hallmark of Frank's artistry was the spontaneity made possible by his handheld 35mm Leica camera, which allowed him to shoot from the hip **[FIG. 4]**. Many photographs in *The Americans* are characterized by visible grain, blurriness, or an off-center composition, qualities that in the 1950s were more often associated with amateur snapshots than with professional photography, but which Frank embraced for their connotations of improvisation or indifference. Yet in *Trolley* he captured his subject with impressive clarity. He may have exposed the film while the vehicle was stopped: the contact sheet reveals a second streetcar image, the main characteristics of which are a blur of illegible faces and the washed-out glare of sunlight on metal siding. By the subsequent frame, Frank had turned away.

The Americans did not include any editorializing captions, nor was it buttressed by deep sociological research, and many of Frank's contemporaries would not have considered him a political photographer. But, looking back, Frank said of *The Americans*, "It was very political. It really talked about that period in America—it showed that period in an unmistakable way, how I felt about it, where I stood."[6] Others—including the Beat writer Jack Kerouac in his introduction to the book—used the word "poetry" to describe Frank's work, validating it as art over and above its use as a social document: "Robert Frank . . . sucked a sad poem right out of America onto film, taking rank among the tragic poets of the world."[7]

Prior to the release of his book, Frank published a selection of photographs from his extended road trip—*Trolley* among them—in the *1958 U.S. Camera Annual*. In a statement accompanying the images (many of which did not appear in *The Americans*), Frank explained his straightforward goals: "With these photographs, I have attempted to show a cross-section of the American population. My effort was to express it simply and without confusion."[8] In *Trolley* this clarity is at least partly achieved through the relative evenness of tone across all the faces in the composition. Sid Kaplan, a printer who frequently worked with Frank, remembered him saying, "It doesn't matter if it's not a good print, as long as it's even."[9] Above the passengers, a rhythmic tapestry of swirling shapes is reflected in the glass, the web of illegible forms contrasting with the row of figures below. That row evokes a film strip, with one frame following another, prompting us to read them in sequence. It is also a collection of pictures within a bigger picture, each component a remarkable image in itself. Marked by a row of vertical white bars, the formal arrangement can also be compared to a prison: the window frames delineate the cells that isolate *Trolley*'s riders from each other and from the bustling world of the street below.

On November 7, 1955, two days before his thirty-first birthday, Frank was pulled over while driving on U.S. Route 65 in the town of McGehee, Arkansas.[10] A letter sent the next month from one of the arresting lieutenants to the police captain in Little Rock reported that Frank had been "shabbily dressed, needed a shave and haircut, also a bath. Subject talked with a foreign accent."[11] The lieutenant also took note of Frank's belongings—cameras, numerous papers in various languages—and arrested him on suspicion of spying. He was fingerprinted and questioned for hours by the authorities, including a local counterintelligence specialist. When he was finally released, around midnight, Frank drove south. Two days later, writing from Port Gibson, Mississippi, to the photographer Walker Evans—his friend and mentor—he called the ordeal "the most humiliating experience I had so far."[12]

The trauma was lasting: the officers' prejudice and their suspicion of his Jewishness made a deep impression on Frank. And, as he recounted in a 1975 lecture, the experience influenced his work:

> I was driving early in the morning on a little country road, and the cops came, stopped my car, and said, "What are you doing?" I said, "I'm on a Guggenheim Fellowship, and I'm traveling around photographing the country." The guy said, "Guggenheim? Who is that?" So they pulled me in. They said, "We got to arrest you," and I said, "What for?" and they said, "Never mind." . . . I didn't know anybody; they could have killed me. It's pretty scary, and I think that somehow came through in the photographs—that violence I was confronted with.[13]

Many years later, in his autobiographical artist's book *The Lines of My Hand*, first published in 1972, Frank reproduced a grid of photographs shot in Port Gibson on the day he wrote to Evans **[FIG. 5]**. The pictures depict a group of white boys gathered by the local high school; it is clear from their dialogue with the photographer, transcribed on the page, that they viewed him with both suspicion and derision.

Frank had acknowledged his position as an outsider—"a European eye [looking] at the United States"—even before he set forth on his trip. In his application for the Guggenheim Fellowship, he wrote, "What I have in mind, then, is observation and record of what one naturalized American finds to see in the United States that signifies the kind of civilization born here and spreading elsewhere."[14] Yet the episode in Arkansas was a turning point; what Frank endured on that day was, for many, what life in the United States is really like. After his experience in McGehee, his pictures took on a different cast, and, as he later recalled, when he photographed the streetcar in New Orleans four days later, he "knew what to look for."[15]

—

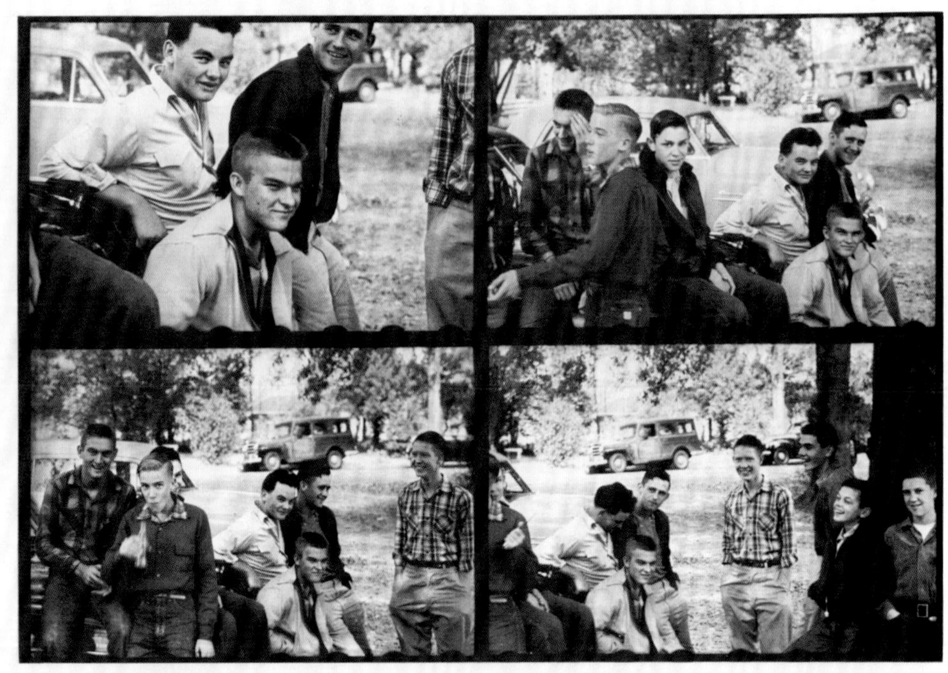

Port Gibson, Mississippi; in front of the Highschool September 1955

Kids: What are you doing here? Are you from New York?
Me: I'm just taking pictures.
Kids: Why?
Me: For myself—just to see.
Kids: He must be a communist. He looks like one. Why don't you go to the other side of town and watch the niggers play?

FIG. 5. *Port Gibson, Mississippi* in Robert Frank's *The Lines of My Hand* (New York: Lustrum, 1972), n.p. Though dated in the book to September, the photographs were taken in November 1955. THE MUSEUM OF MODERN ART LIBRARY, NEW YORK

Frank was born to a bourgeois Jewish family in Zurich, Switzerland, in 1924. He was drawn to photography early, apprenticing with several professional photographers before emigrating to New York at age twenty-two. He arrived in the city in March 1947 and was hired the next month by Alexey Brodovitch, art director of the influential fashion magazine *Harper's Bazaar*, where he worked full-time for several months before continuing as a freelance photographer.[16] It was Brodovitch who introduced Frank to the 35mm Leica that he began carrying that year, switching from the slower Rolleiflex twin-lens reflex camera he had used in Europe.[17]

Frank also received early recognition from Edward Steichen, the director of the Department of Photography at The Museum of Modern Art. Steichen presented one of Frank's photographs for the first time in an exhibition in 1950 (*Photographs by 51 Photographers*), and in 1955 he included seven photographs by Frank in his influential traveling exhibition *The Family of Man*.[18] Steichen's exhibition was an attempt to trace universal characteristics of humanity across geography, class, and social circumstance, while Frank's subsequent project, *The Americans*, argued against a homogeneous reading of American culture.[19] As Evans put it, Frank's work "is a far cry from all the wooly, successful 'photo-sentiments' about human familyhood."[20]

In New York, Frank was also close with Beat writers and poets and Abstract Expressionist painters. He identified with their solitary pursuit of art, their outlaw status, and their rejection of popular views and behavior. "I didn't know any people in Europe that lived like that," he recollected later. "They were free, and that impressed me. They paid no attention to how you dressed or where you lived. They made their own rules."[21] At the same time, Frank benefitted from the esteem of establishment figures. His application for the Guggenheim Fellowship, submitted in October 1954, included recommendations from Brodovitch and Steichen; Evans, who besides his accomplishment as a photographer was also an editor at *Fortune* magazine; Alexander Liberman, *Vogue*'s art director; and Meyer Schapiro, an art history professor at Columbia University. In April 1955 Frank became the first European photographer to be awarded a Guggenheim Fellowship.

That June, just before setting off for the Midwest on the first leg of his road trip, Frank used part of the grant money to purchase a 1950 Ford Business Coupe. This car, his constant companion on the road, is pictured in the last photograph in *The Americans, U.S. 90, En Route to Del Rio, Texas* **[FIG. 6]**. The image, in which Frank's wife Mary can be seen huddled in the Ford's front seat together with their young son, Pablo (their daughter, Andrea, was also in the car), is a poignant bookend to *Trolley*. In *Trolley* Frank looked at a streetcar from outside, capturing a cross-section of Americans but also the divisions between them. In *U.S. 90* Frank was also looking in, but this time he was looking at his own family; this is his personal view. In his initial statement accompanying the photographs that make

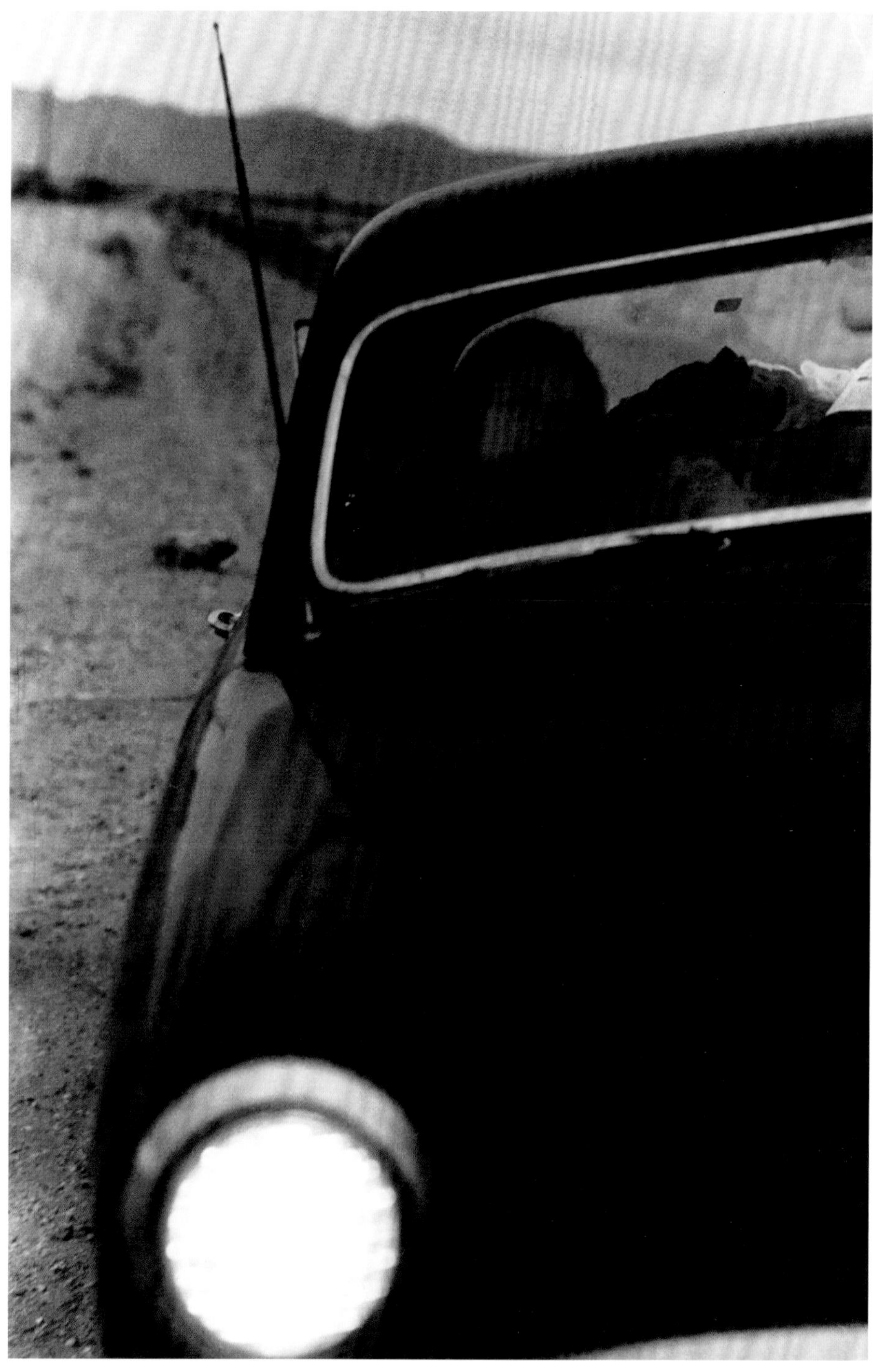

FIG. 6. Robert Frank (American, born Switzerland. 1924–2019). *U.S. 90, En Route to Del Rio, Texas.* 1955. Gelatin silver print, 12 11/16 × 8 3/8" (32.2 × 21.3 cm). THE MUSEUM OF MODERN ART, NEW YORK. PURCHASE

up *The Americans*, Frank emphasized that the images were the result not only of objective observation, but also of his own perspective: "It is important to see what is invisible to others. Perhaps the look of hope or the look of sadness. Also it is always the instantaneous reaction to oneself that produces a photograph."[22] In observing the world, Frank recognized his own position in it.

—

By early 1957 Frank had compiled more than twenty thousand images on nearly eight hundred rolls of film. He refined this mass into a group of fewer than one hundred images, producing maquettes to finesse the sequence for the book. Frank could not initially find an American publisher, and, as he had anticipated, the pictures were distributed first in Europe.[23] In November 1958, Robert Delpire released *Les Américains* in France **[FIGS. 7, 8]**.

The book was the fifth title in Delpire's series Encyclopédie Essentielle, which offered edited, rather than exhaustive, surveys on cultural and anthropological subjects. The eighty-three photographs were printed as gravures by Draeger Frères, a storied French printer, and bound alongside excerpts from texts by various authors selected by Alain Bosquet, a poet and critic. Printed in French, these range from the political (Abraham Lincoln, Harry S. Truman) to the literary (Simone de Beauvoir, William Faulkner), on subjects including nationalism and inequality. The experience of race is a consistent theme, as in, for example, Langston Hughes's 1926 poem "Cross" ("I wonder where I'm gonna die / Being neither white nor black?"). Frank's photographs were printed on the right-hand page of each spread, as full-page images, and the excerpts appear facing them. While the relationships between image and text seem somewhat haphazard, the juxtapositions raise new readings. *Charleston, South Carolina* **[FIG. 9]**, for example, appears across from the United States Declaration of Independence, prompting consideration of how the nation's promise of equality was fulfilled in the lives of the two Americans in the picture.

The first two maquettes Frank made for the book were labeled "America" and "America, America," but in the end the volume was given a title that refers to the people rather than the place. Curator Sarah Greenough has suggested that this may have been an intentional echo of Henri Cartier-Bresson's album *Les Européens* (The Europeans), which was published in 1955; the French photographer had been an early influence on Frank.[24] Subsequent titles in Delpire's series used the same format, such as *Les Arabes* (The Arabs, 1959) and *Les Allemands* (The Germans, 1963).

The cover of *Les Américains* features a cityscape by illustrator Saul Steinberg, depicting miniature pedestrians in an imagined urban landscape. Frank felt that this whimsical design was not right for the book. In a letter to publisher Barney Rosset, whose Grove Press (a New York–based alternative press associated with

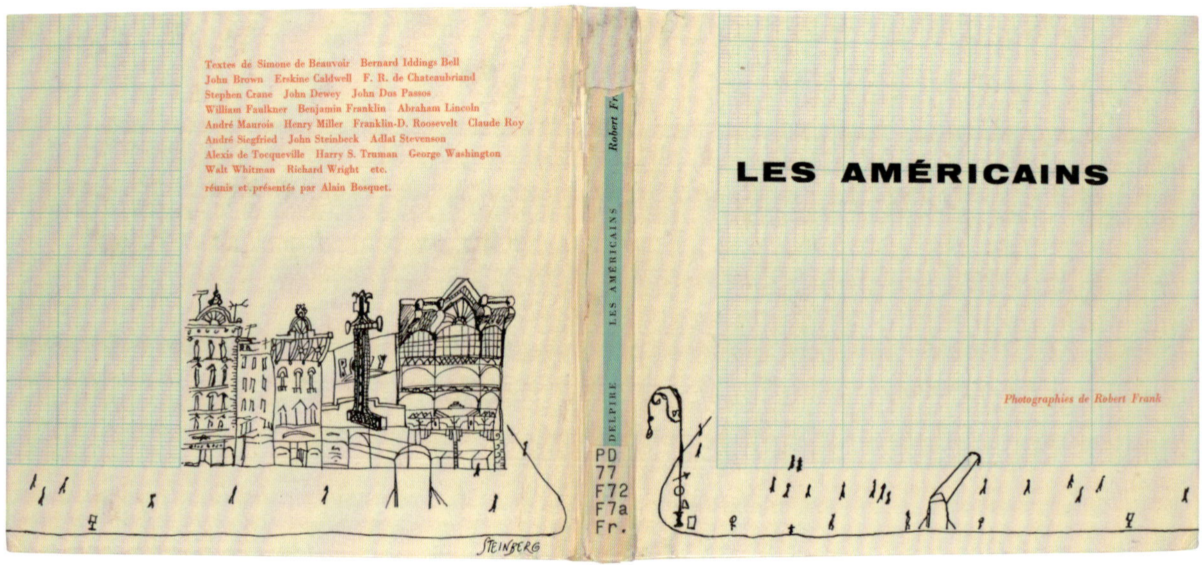

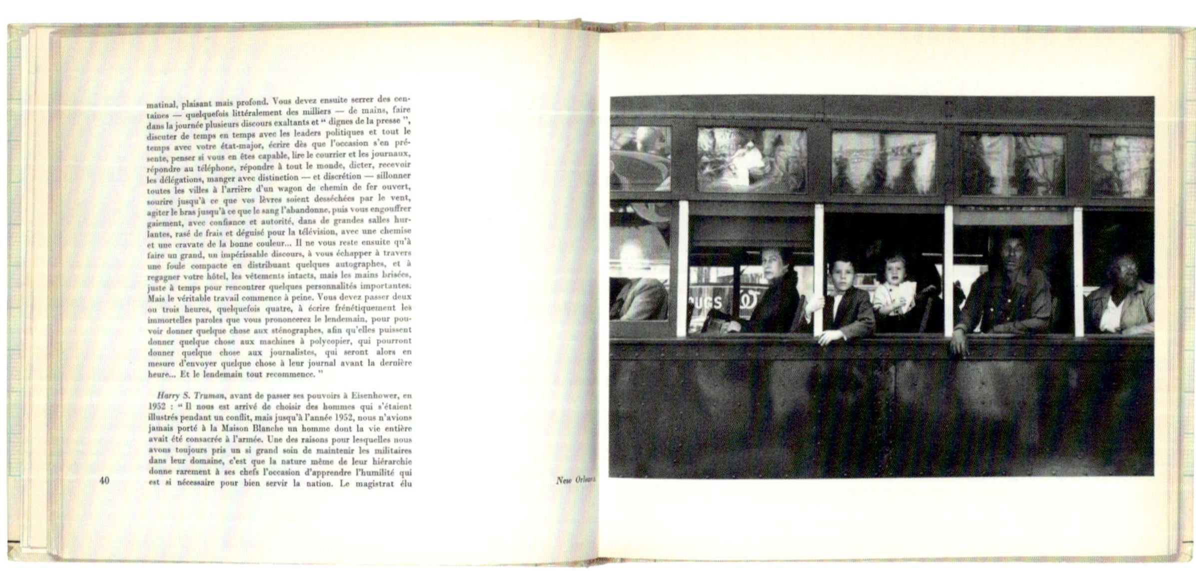

matinal, plaisant mais profond. Vous devez ensuite serrer des centaines — quelquefois littéralement des milliers — de mains, faire dans la journée plusieurs discours exaltants et « dignes de la presse », discuter de temps en temps avec les leaders politiques et tout le temps avec votre état-major, écrire dès que l'occasion s'en présente, penser si vous en êtes capable, lire le courrier et les journaux, répondre au téléphone, répondre à tout le monde, dicter, recevoir les délégations, manger avec distinction — et discrétion — sillonner toutes les villes à l'arrière d'un wagon de chemin de fer ouvert, sourire jusqu'à ce que vos lèvres soient desséchées par le vent, agiter le bras jusqu'à ce que le sang l'abandonne, puis vous engouffrer gaiement, avec confiance et autorité, dans de grandes salles hurlantes, rasé de frais et déguisé pour la télévision, avec une chemise et une cravate de la bonne couleur... Il ne vous reste ensuite qu'à faire un grand, un impérissable discours, à vous échapper à travers une foule compacte en distribuant quelques autographes, et à regagner votre hôtel, les vêtements intacts, mais les mains brisées, juste à temps pour rencontrer quelques personnalités importantes. Mais le véritable travail commence à peine. Vous devez passer deux ou trois heures, quelquefois quatre, à écrire frénétiquement les immortelles paroles que vous prononcerez le lendemain, pour pouvoir donner quelque chose aux sténographes, afin qu'elles puissent donner quelque chose aux machines à polycopier, qui pourront donner quelque chose aux journalistes, qui seront alors en mesure d'envoyer quelque chose à leur journal avant la dernière heure... Et le lendemain tout recommence. »

Harry S. Truman, avant de passer ses pouvoirs à Eisenhower, en 1952 : « Il nous est arrivé de choisir des hommes qui s'étaient illustrés pendant un conflit, mais jusqu'à l'année 1952, nous n'avions jamais porté à la Maison Blanche un homme dont la vie entière avait été consacrée à l'armée. Une des raisons pour lesquelles nous avons toujours pris un si grand soin de maintenir les militaires dans leur domaine, c'est que la nature même de leur hiérarchie donne rarement à ses chefs l'occasion d'apprendre l'humilité qui est si nécessaire pour bien servir la nation. Le magistrat élu

40

New Orleans

FIGS. 7, 8. *Les Américains* (Paris: Delpire, 1958), jacket and pages 40–41. Jacket illustration by Saul Steinberg. Page 41: Robert Frank, *Trolley—New Orleans*. THE MUSEUM OF MODERN ART LIBRARY, NEW YORK

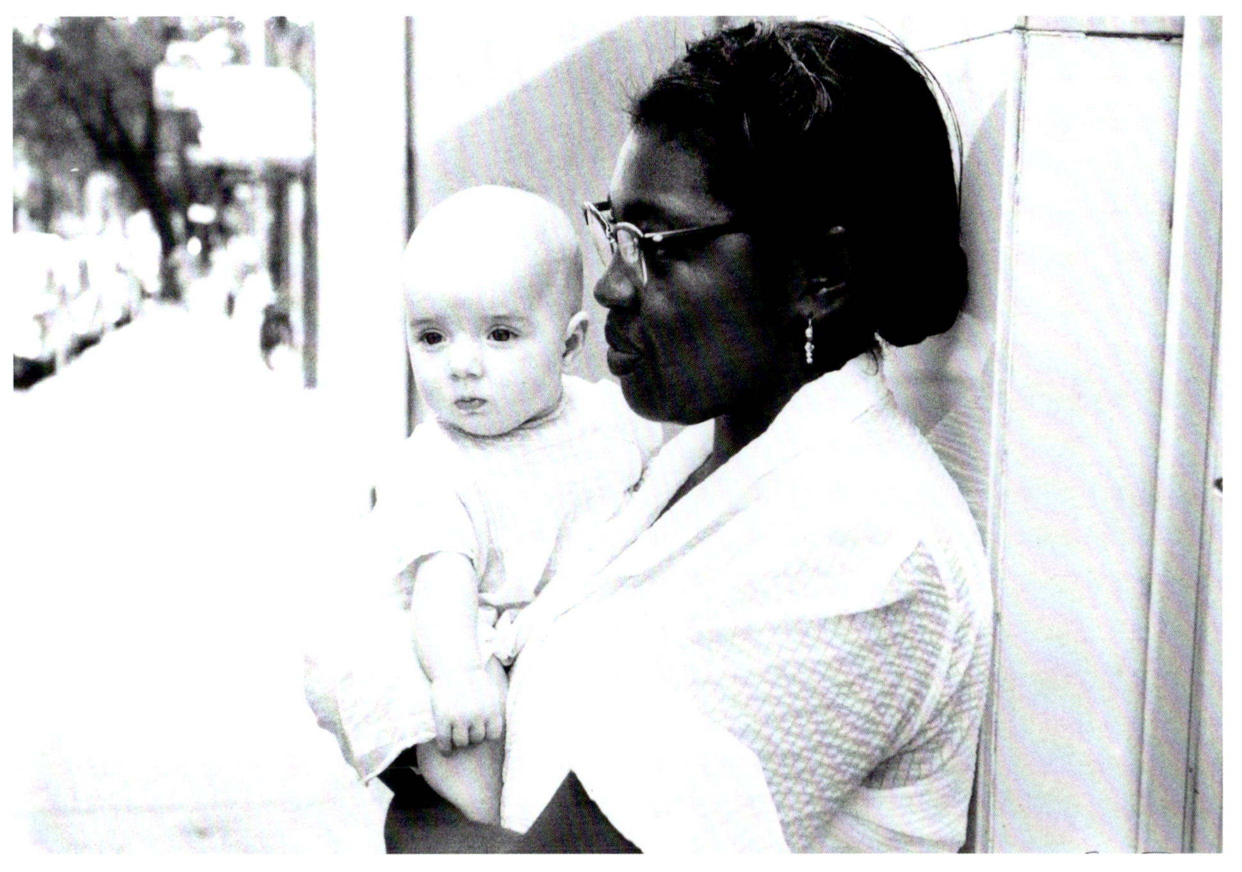

FIG. 9. Robert Frank (American, born Switzerland. 1924–2019) *Charleston, South Carolina*. 1955. Gelatin silver print, 12 ¼ × 18 ¼" (31.1 × 46.3 cm). THE MUSEUM OF MODERN ART, NEW YORK. GIFT OF ROBERT AND GAYLE GREENHILL

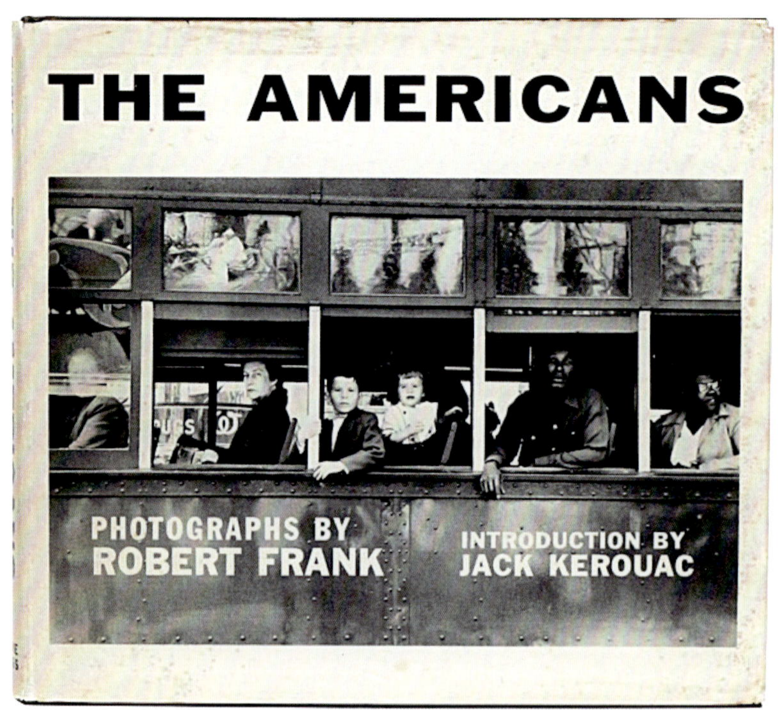

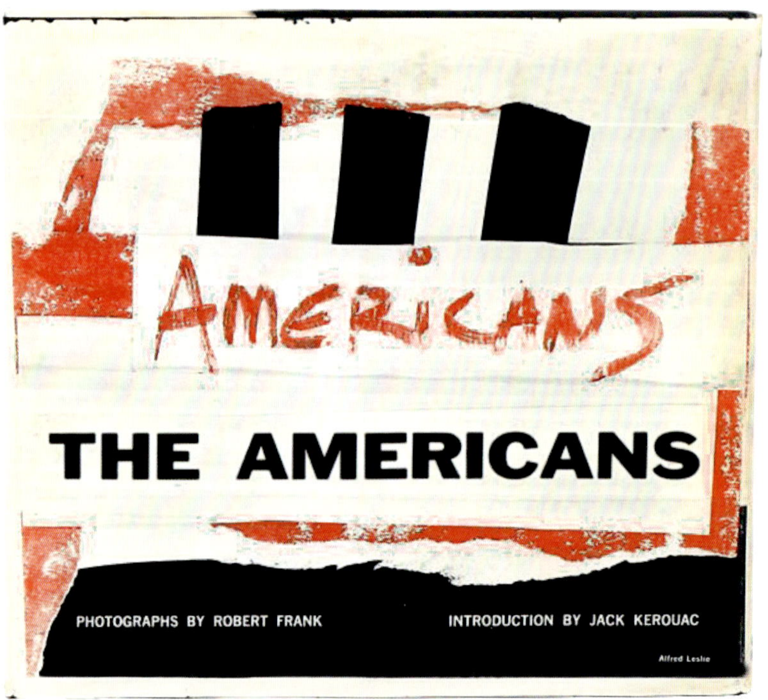

FIGS. 10, 11. *The Americans* (New York: Grove, 1959), front and back covers. Front: Robert Frank, *Trolley—New Orleans.* Back: illustration by Alfred Leslie

the Beats and other avant-garde literature) agreed to take on the American edition of the book, he suggested asking Willem de Kooning or Franz Kline—Abstract Expressionist painters—to design the cover.[25] The eventual design for the American edition did incorporate on its back cover a drawing by the Abstract Expressionist Alfred Leslie, Frank's friend and collaborator. Its vertical black-and-white stripes rhyme visually with *Trolley,* on the front cover **[FIGS. 10, 11]**. About the decision to feature *Trolley*, Frank later said, "It seemed to be the right picture. It expressed a lot of what I'd seen on the trip. A treatment of Black people. I felt it really reflected some of the strongest moments on my trip. When I experienced for the first time segregation, it was important to me that it could be expressed like this."[26]

Grove bought Draeger Frères' remaining reproductions of Frank's photographs and bound them with a simple title on each left-hand page, as was Frank's preference, and added the introduction by Kerouac, eliminating the excerpted texts Delpire had included. On January 15, 1960, *The Americans* was released in the United States, where it received immediate critical attention.[27] In their introduction to a collection of responses to the book, the editors of *Popular Photography* noted the mixed quality of the reviews: "Seldom has a book of photographs aroused as much controversy in the *Popular Photography* office as Robert Frank's *The Americans*. . . . The reactions of the editors ranged from admiration to contempt."[28] The criticism addressed the photographs' style (Arthur Goldsmith wrote that the pictures were "flawed by meaningless blur, grain, muddy exposure, drunken horizons and general sloppiness") and subject matter (Les Barry claimed the book was "an attack on the United States"), while others were impressed by Frank's unique vision (H. M. Kinzer commended his "sharp perception").[29]

Despite its presence on the cover of the book, reviews from 1960 do not tend to mention *Trolley*, but many writers addressed Frank's depiction of the lives of Black Americans in other photographs, such as *Charleston, South Carolina*, which was made in the summer of 1955, prior to Frank's time in New Orleans. Of that leg of the trip, in which he and Mary drove south through the Carolinas and Georgia, he said, "It was the first time I was in the South, and the first time I really saw segregation. I found it extraordinary that whites would give their children to black women when they wouldn't allow the women to sit by them in the drugstore."[30] The photograph that Frank regularly cited as his favorite in the book, *San Francisco* **[FIG. 12]**, also makes a point about relationships between Black and white people in America. A Black man and woman, lounging together in a park, look straight at the camera, their expressions captured at the moment they realize they are being watched. Calling the picture "racially fraught" in a piece for the *New York Times* in 2015, art historian Maurice Berger pointed out that a photographer like Frank was not a neutral observer but rather—like the

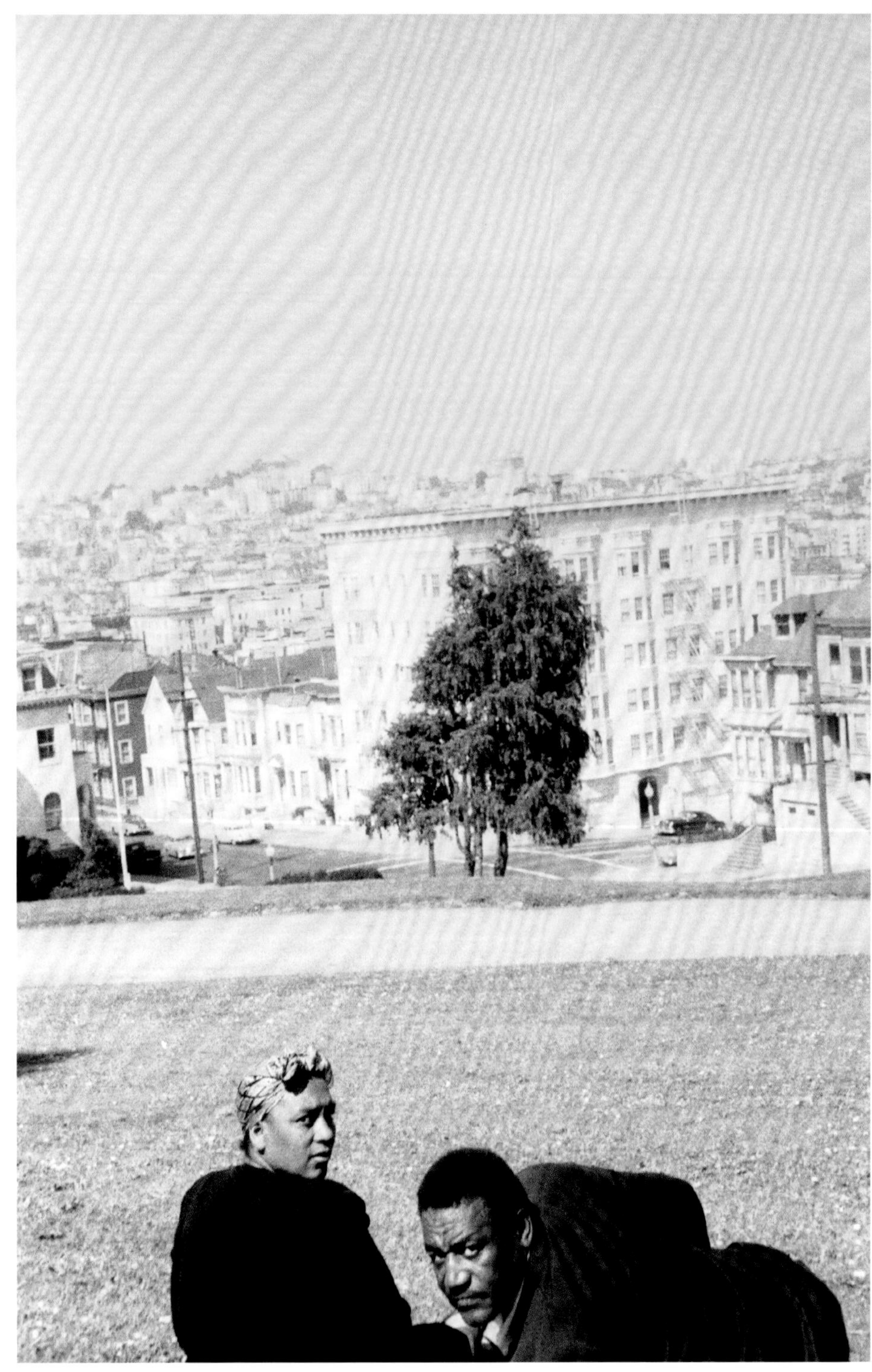

FIG. 12. Robert Frank (American, born Switzerland. 1924–2019). *San Francisco*. 1955. Gelatin silver print, 11 x 14" (27.9 x 35.6 cm)

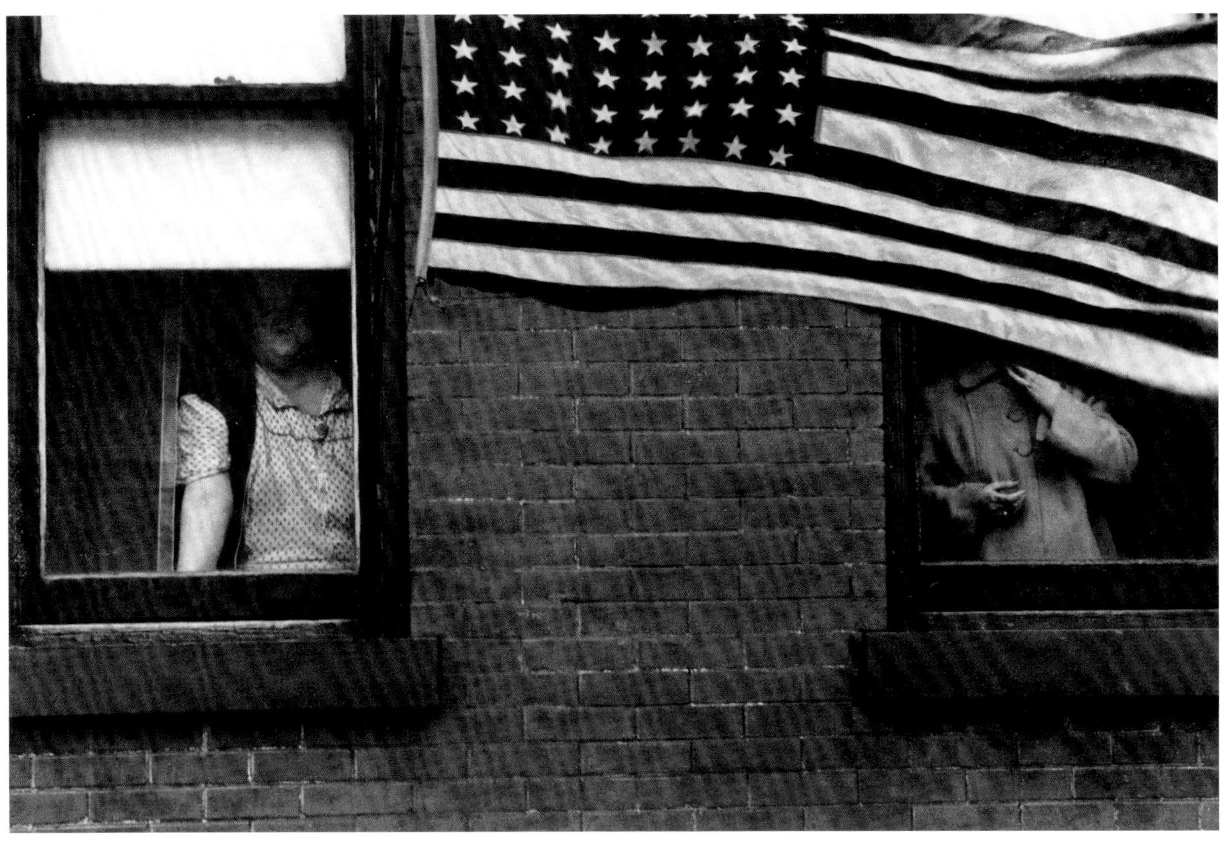

FIG. 13. Robert Frank (American, born Switzerland. 1924–2019). *Parade—Hoboken, New Jersey*. 1955. Gelatin silver print, 8 1⁄16 × 12 1⁄4" (20.5 × 31.1 cm). THE MUSEUM OF MODERN ART, NEW YORK. PURCHASE

viewer—"a surrogate for the intimidating whiteness that shadowed the lives of black Americans, no matter how liberal their environment."[31]

Other photographs in *The Americans* echo elements of *Trolley*'s composition, if not (or at least, not overtly) its observation of racial inequity. The first picture in the book, *Parade—Hoboken, New Jersey* **[FIG. 13]**, appearing just after Kerouac's introduction, was also one of the first photographs Frank made for this body of work, taken before he set out on his road trip. The image has several characteristics that are hallmarks of the book overall: it is one of many photographs in which the American flag is a scrim or a visual barrier, and, as in *Trolley*, the windows in the composition serve as framing devices that isolate individuals from each other and from the world outside.

In *U.S. 91, Leaving Blackfoot, Idaho* **[FIG. 14]**, Frank has joined the cast of figures who look outward. He shares the front seat of his Ford with two hitchhikers,

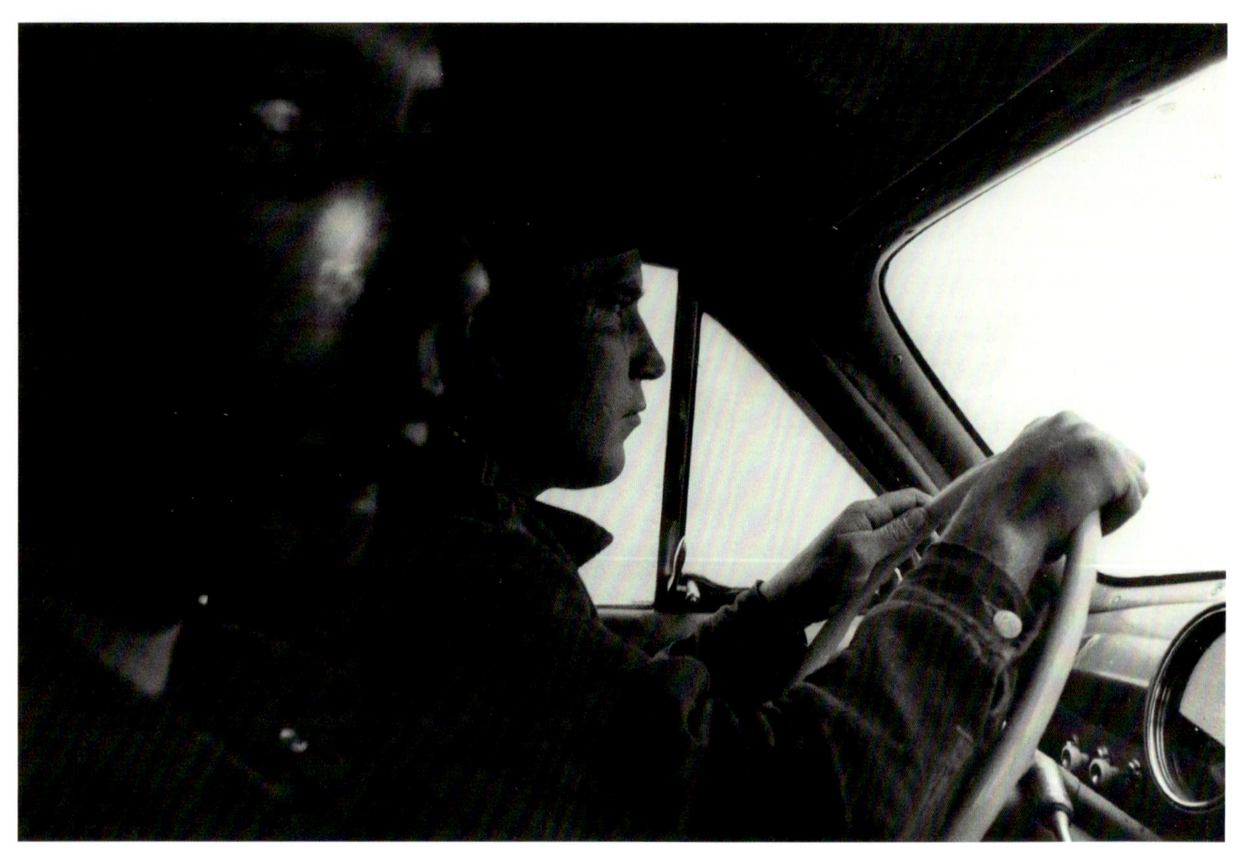

FIG. 14. Robert Frank (American, born Switzerland. 1924–2019). *U.S. 91, Leaving Blackfoot, Idaho*. 1956. Gelatin silver print, 6 ¼ x 13 ¾" (15.9 × 34.9 cm). NATIONAL GALLERY OF ART, WASHINGTON, D.C. ROBERT FRANK COLLECTION. GIFT OF ROBERT FRANK

one of whom has taken the wheel. Not only is he no longer observing from outside, but he has also provided some measure of liberation to the two young men, who appear to be heading into an expanse of blankness; the world is wide open to them. On a piece of paper clipped under the sunshade, we can barely make out a short text by the philosopher Francis Bacon: "The contemplation of things as they are, without error or confusion, without substitution or imposture, is in itself a nobler thing, than a whole harvest of invention." Frank encountered this quotation while visiting the photographer Dorothea Lange, who had tacked it to her darkroom door in Berkeley, California, and the words are a clue to the influence of social documentary photography like Lange's on *The Americans*.[32] They are also a foreshadowing of the significance that pictures like *Trolley* would assume in the American civil rights movement: in contemplating "things as they are," Frank made images that exposed the fundamental inequalities of his time.

Photography played a crucial role in the civil rights movement. Photographs possess an inherent power of persuasion: confronted with the images circulating in their newspapers, Northern whites could no longer ignore the segregation prevalent in the Jim Crow South—or ignore the great risks many people were taking to protest such injustices. New Orleans, where *Trolley* was made, was the site of many defining pictures from the civil rights era. Five years after Frank passed through, for example, newspapers around the country printed photographs of young Ruby Bridges on the steps of the city's William Frantz Elementary School, accompanied by U.S. Marshals as she became the first Black child to attend the all-white school **[FIG. 15]**. Photographer Leonard Freed was still documenting blatant segregation in the city three years later, creating images for his book *Black in White America*, a cross-country investigation of the struggles and joys of Black life **[FIG. 16]**.

Frank's contact sheets reveal that initially he, like Freed, photographed the "white" and "colored" signs that were ubiquitous across the South, but as his trip progressed he became less drawn to such straightforward representations of discrimination.[33] Instead he tended to capture the conditions in which his subjects lived without the obvious markers of segregation. Photographer Elliott Erwitt **[FIG. 17]**, an early friend of Frank's, described the differences in their approaches: Unlike Frank, he said, "I became a professional doing what people expected from me. . . . I felt he felt I'd gone the wrong way, the nonartist way."[34]

In 1964 a cropped version of *Trolley* was included among many other photographs in a landmark book compiled by the Student Nonviolent Coordinating Committee (SNCC)—an independent activist group formed in 1960 with encouragement from the Southern Christian Leadership Conference—to support and advance its work in the cause of civil rights. *The Movement: Documentary of a Struggle*

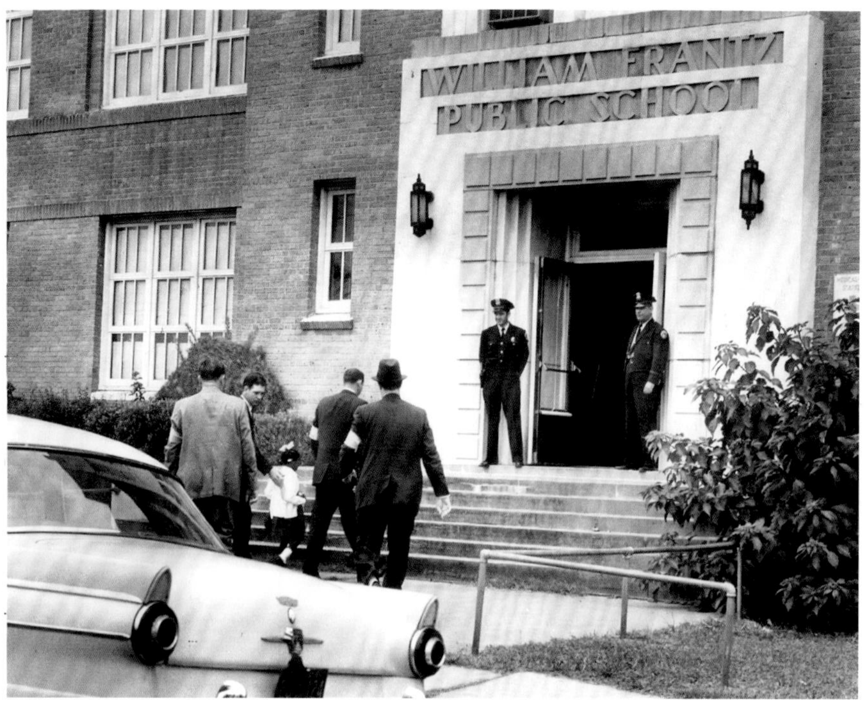

FIG. 15. Ruby Bridges with U.S. Marshals at William Frantz Elementary School, New Orleans, November 14, 1960. Photo: Frank Methe. TIMES-PICAYUNE ARCHIVE, NEW ORLEANS

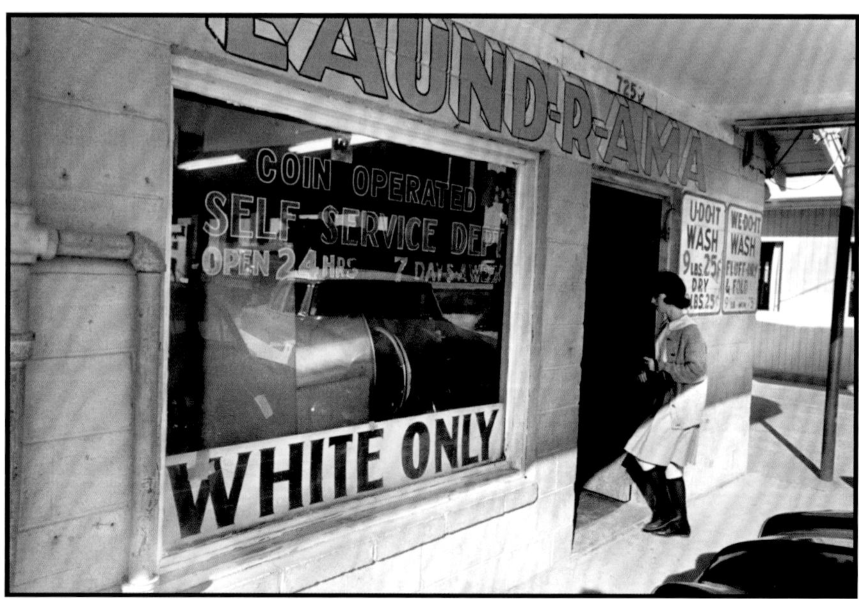

FIG. 16. Leonard Freed (American, 1929–2006). *New Orleans: A woman entering a segregated laundromat—white only*. 1963

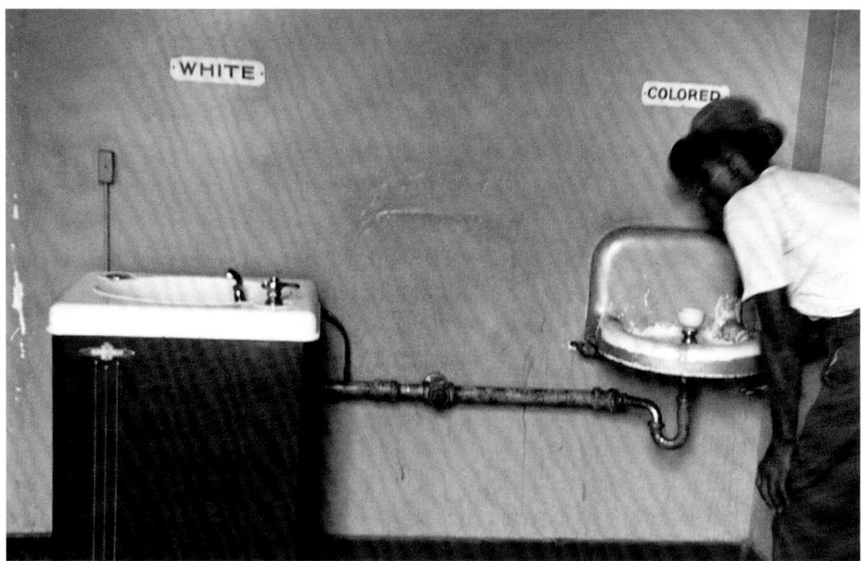

FIG. 17. Elliott Erwitt (American, born France 1928). *Wilmington, North Carolina*. 1950. Gelatin silver print, 8 11/16 × 13 ½" (22.1 × 34.3 cm). THE MUSEUM OF MODERN ART, NEW YORK. GIFT OF THE ARTIST

for Equality **[FIG. 18]** was shepherded at the publisher Simon & Schuster by the editor Elizabeth Sutherland, who—under her given name, Betita Martínez—went on to be a prominent Chicana activist. In 1957–58 Sutherland had been Steichen's assistant in the Department of Photography at MoMA, and it was there that she became familiar with Frank and his work. Danny Lyon, the first staff photographer at SNCC (and later a close friend of Frank's), took most of the photographs reproduced in *The Movement* and worked closely with Sutherland to compile the others.

The book puts the civil rights movement into a wider context through images from across the country's history, ranging from horrific photographs of lynchings to uplifting portraits of young protesters. Many of the pictures, including the cover image by Lyon, depict violence against Black Americans at the hands of white law enforcement or white civilians in the South. Historian Martin A. Berger has argued that while such pictures elicit sympathy, they also preserve detrimental racial hierarchies and reassure whites of their own power: "For white audiences, such images are perversely safe to look at, because they create distance between the perpetrators of violence and those who witness it."[35] Frank's *Trolley*, on the other hand, demonstrates the manner in which ordinary people cooperated in maintaining white supremacy through the commonplace activities of their everyday lives.[36] Even the young girl, with her hand on the race screen, is implicated.

In *The Movement*, *Trolley* shares a spread with a United Press International photograph, taken during the 1943 Detroit race riots, in which a group of white

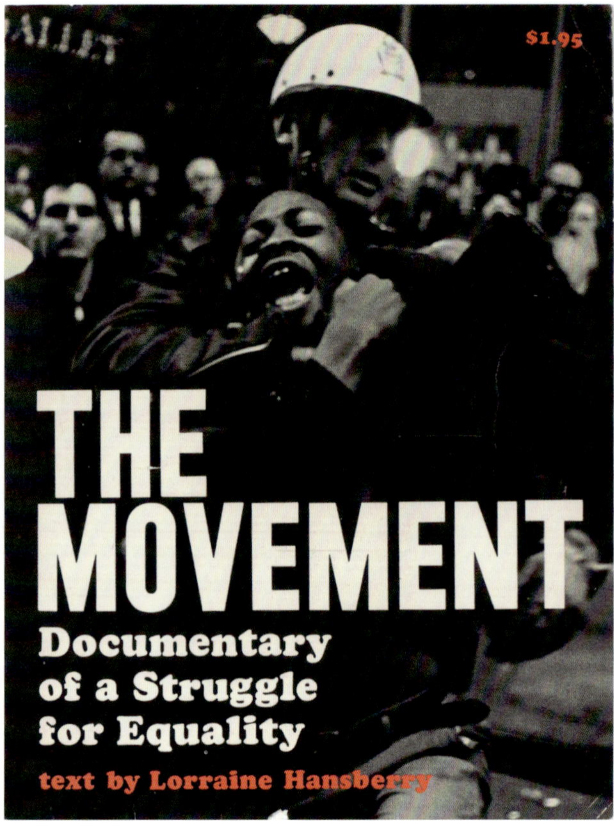

FIG. 18. *The Movement: Documentary of a Struggle for Equality* (New York: Simon & Schuster, 1964). Cover photograph: Danny Lyon, *Atlanta, Georgia—High school student Taylor Washington is arrested at Lebs Delicatessen—His eighth arrest*, 1963 or 1964. THE MUSEUM OF MODERN ART LIBRARY, NEW YORK

men surround a Black man on a city street **[FIG. 19]**. The pages that directly precede and follow this spread include a mix of portraits and images made in both rural and urban settings, along with these lines by the playwright Lorraine Hansberry, who wrote the text for the book: "The laws which enforce segregation do not presume the inferiority of a people; they assume an inherent equalness. It is the logic of the lawmakers that if a society does not erect artificial barriers between the people at every point of contact, the people might fraternize and give their attention to the genuine, shared problems of the community."[37] It was these barriers that the civil rights movement sought to destroy. A few pages later, the text continues: "On February 1, 1960, four Negro students sat down at the 'white only' lunch counter of the Woolworth store in Greensboro, North Carolina. What followed is changing the entire nation."[38]

—

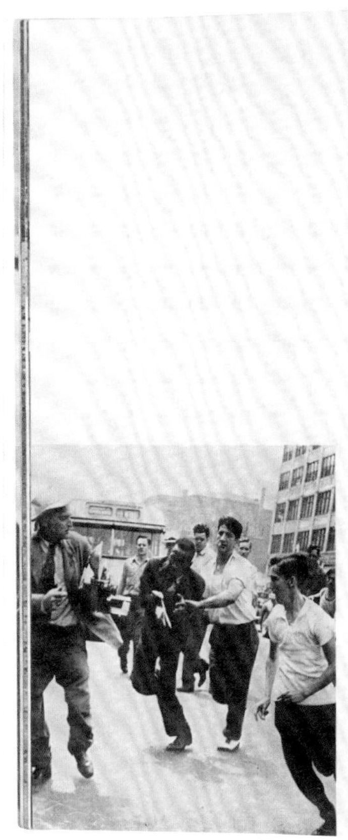

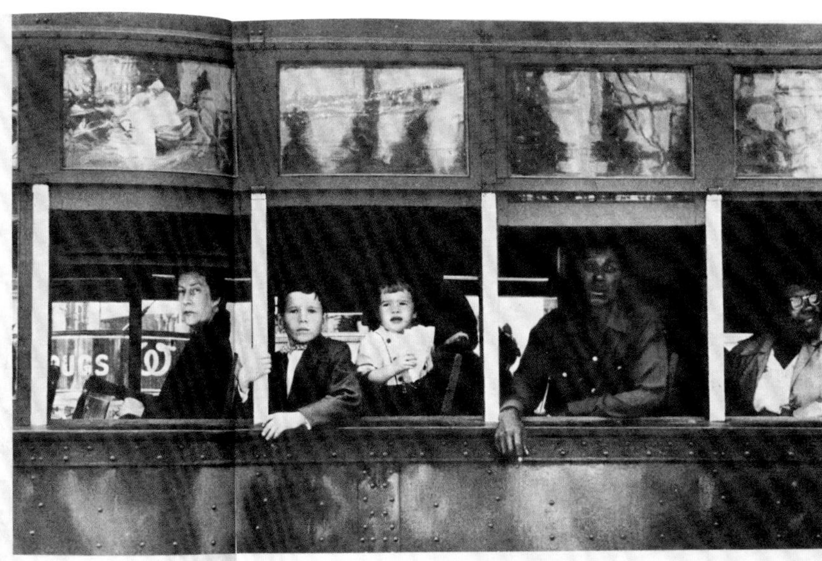

FIG. 19. *The Movement: Documentary of a Struggle for Equality* (New York: Simon & Schuster, 1964), pages 28–29. At left: United Press International, *Detroit*, 1943. At right: Robert Frank, *Trolley—New Orleans*.
THE MUSEUM OF MODERN ART LIBRARY, NEW YORK

In *Trolley* the word "DRUGS" and a distinctive "W" logotype are partially visible behind the streetcar, painted on the windows across the street. These signs mark a bustling location of the national drugstore chain Walgreens, located on the corner of New Orleans's Canal and Baronne Streets. Several months after the sit-ins in Greensboro—and almost two years after Frank made *Trolley*—a group of Black and white students associated with the Congress for Racial Equality staged sit-ins at the segregated lunch counters of this Walgreens and the nearby Woolworth's store **[FIG. 20]**, refusing to leave until the Black students were served. These and the many other lunch-counter sit-ins held throughout the South in the early 1960s attracted extensive media attention, and besides leading to the integration of dining rooms and other facilities, they galvanized others to join the movement. As a form of protest, sit-ins were explicitly nonviolent, although violence did on occasion arise: at the Canal Street Walgreens,

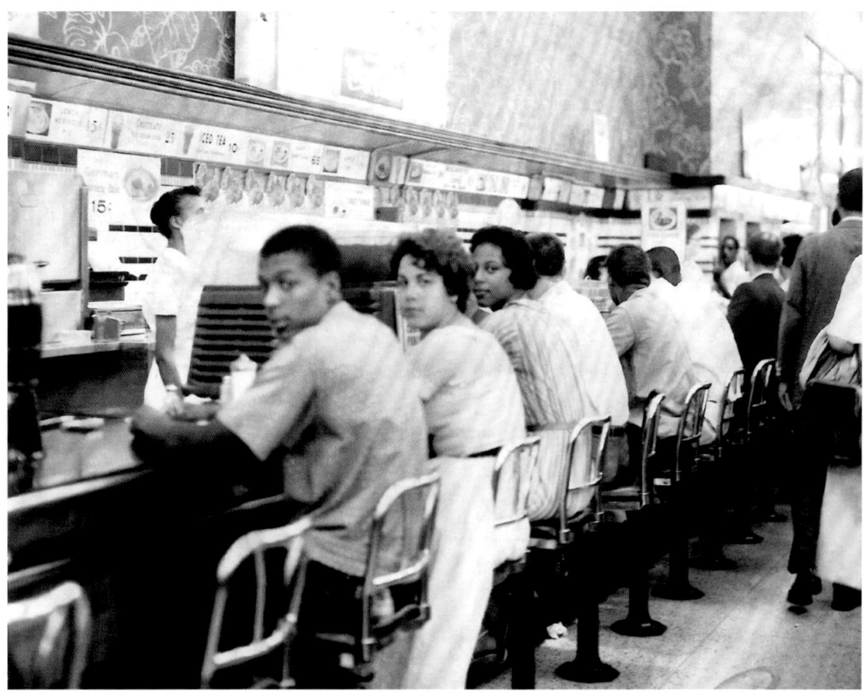

FIG. 20. Sit-in by members of the Congress for Racial Equality at Woolworth's lunch counter, Canal Street, New Orleans, September 9, 1960. Photo: Ralph Uribe. TIMES-PICAYUNE ARCHIVE, NEW ORLEANS

a participant reported, a waitress "served the black patrons at the counter, but then smashed all the dishes they had eaten from."[39]

For many viewers, the drugstore lunch counter was a symbol of 1950s American culture, and Frank included them in *The Americans* alongside jukeboxes and barbershops [**FIG. 21**]. Later, after the sit-ins, the lunch counter became a symbol of the segregated South, joining the streetcar and the bus. Key sites of struggle in the fight for equal rights, all three had a history of use by artists conveying life under Jim Crow. Among these artists was Jacob Lawrence, who, in 1941, moved from New York to New Orleans, where he made the painting *Bus* [**FIG. 22**]. "They had the signs that moved up and down when you got on a conveyance, a bus," Lawrence recalled in an interview. "If you were black you sat behind the sign, if you were not black you sat in front."[40] This was one of the everyday injustices that motivated the massive demographic shift Lawrence chronicled in his Migration Series (1940–41), a group of sixty painted panels narrating the journey of Black migrants from the rural South to the cities of the Midwest and the Northeast in the first half of the twentieth century. Later in the decade the photographer Marion Palfi boarded a bus to document inequity in the South up close [**FIG. 23**]. In the 1950s *Life* magazine published a series of features on the topic of segregation in America, including

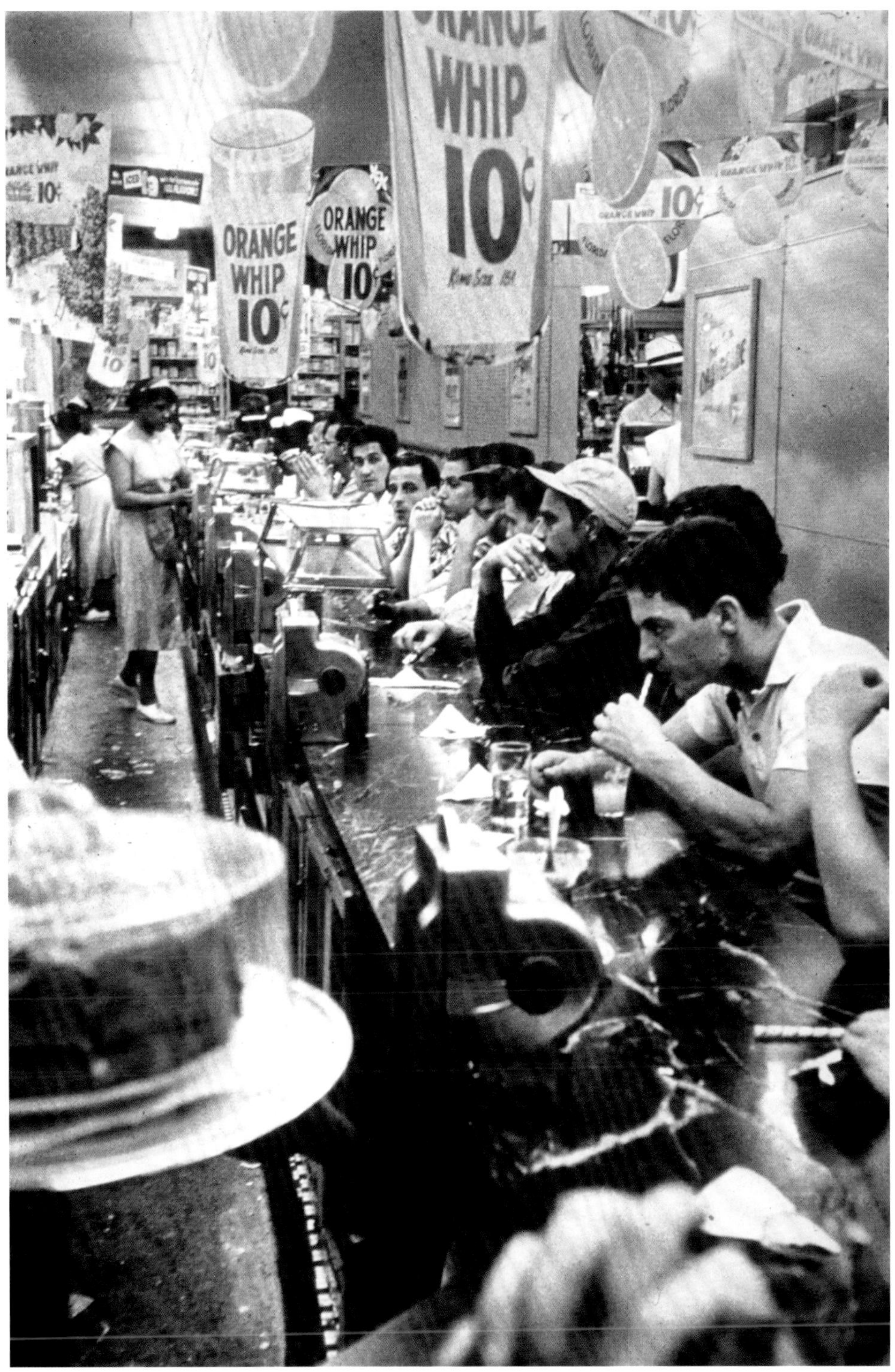

FIG. 21. Robert Frank (American, born Switzerland 1924–2019). *Drugstore—Detroit*. 1955. Gelatin silver print, 11 x 14" (27.9 x 35.6 cm)

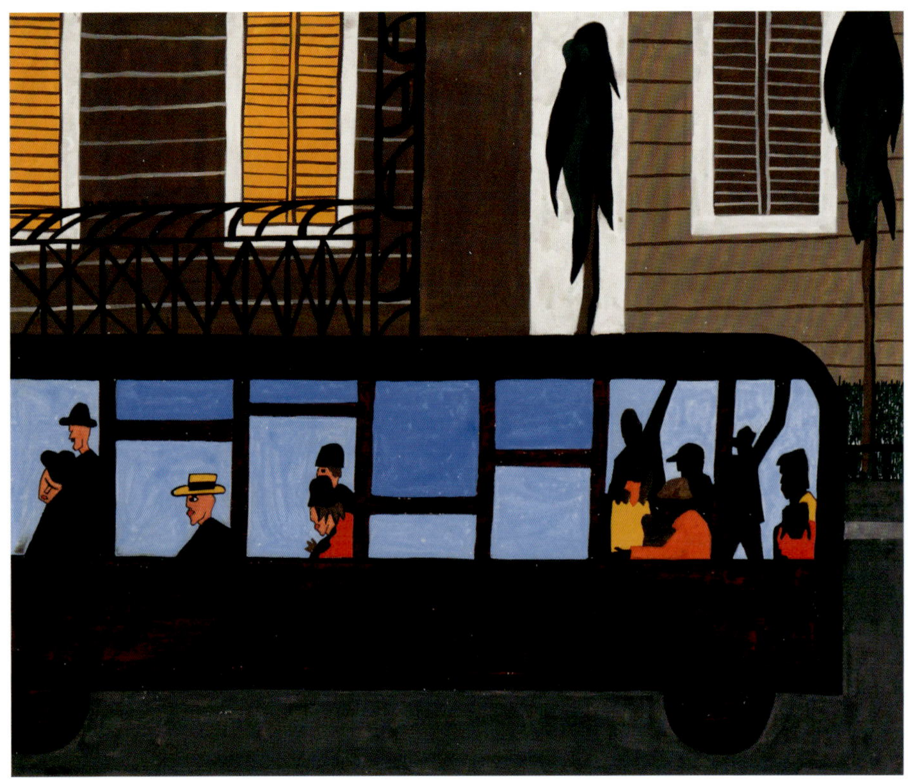

FIG. 22. Jacob Lawrence (American, 1917–2000). *Bus.* 1941. Gouache on paper, 18 5⁄16 x 21 7⁄8" (46.5 x 55.6 cm).
PRIVATE COLLECTION

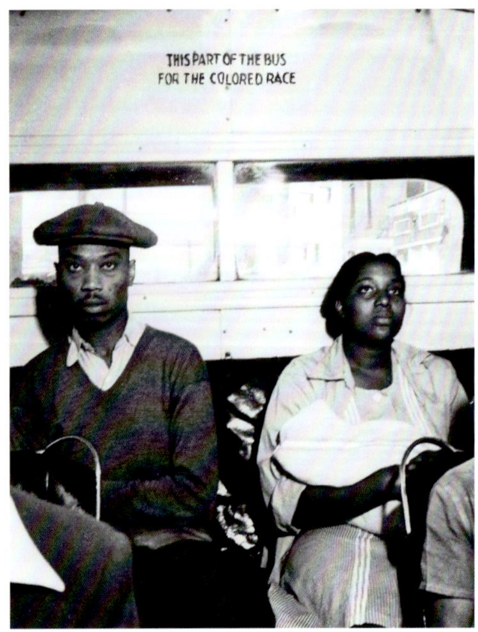

FIG. 23. Marion Palfi (American, born Germany. 1907–1978). *Somewhere in the South. The "Colored" Section at the Back of the Bus.* c. 1946. Gelatin silver print, 9 ½ x 7 ½" (24.2 x 19 cm).
CENTER FOR CREATIVE PHOTOGRAPHY, MARION PALFI ARCHIVE. GIFT OF THE MENNINGER FOUNDATION AND MARTIN MAGNER

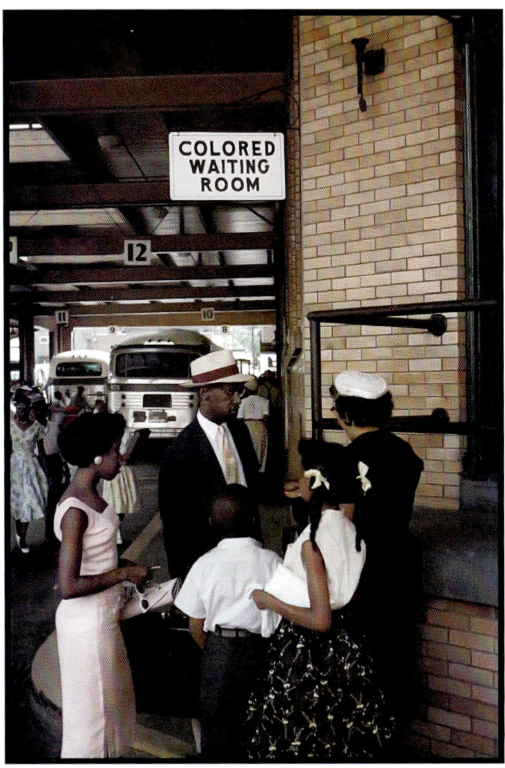

FIG. 24. Gordon Parks (American, 1912–2006). *Untitled, Nashville, Tennessee*. 1956. Published in "The Restraints: Open and Hidden," *Life*, September 24, 1956. Text by Robert Wallace

a photo-essay by Gordon Parks in September 1956 featuring the daily life of an extended Black family in the rural South. Under an image of family members gathered outside a bus station, the caption reads, "Professor Thornton comes face to face with segregation" [**FIG. 24**]. Segregated transportation became the subject of even more frequent documentation in the months leading up to the Montgomery bus boycott, which began in December 1955—a month after Frank made *Trolley*—and lasted more than a year. In photographs commissioned by *Collier's* magazine, Dan Weiner—who, like Palfi, had been a member of the socially conscious cooperative Photo League—captured multiple views of the boycott, from an image of Black would-be passengers awaiting rides by volunteer drivers [**FIG. 25**] to a picture of a lone white rider on an otherwise empty bus, comfortable in the spacious seat, but—hopefully—uncomfortable in her privilege [**FIG. 26**]. Photographers like Ernest C. Withers, who regularly photographed Dr. Martin Luther King, Jr., and other civil rights activists, were there to capture Dr. King and Rev. Ralph Abernathy on the first

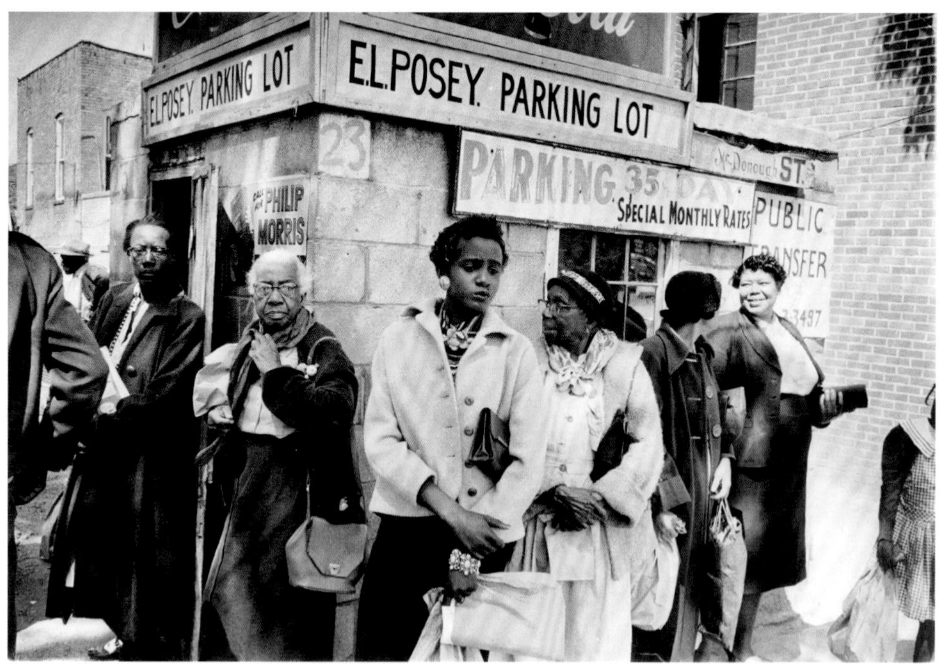

FIG. 25. Dan Weiner (American, 1919–1959). *Bus Boycott, Montgomery, Alabama*. 1956. Gelatin silver print, 10 15⁄16 × 13 15⁄16" (27.8 × 35.5 cm). THE MUSEUM OF MODERN ART, NEW YORK. GIFT OF SANDRA WEINER

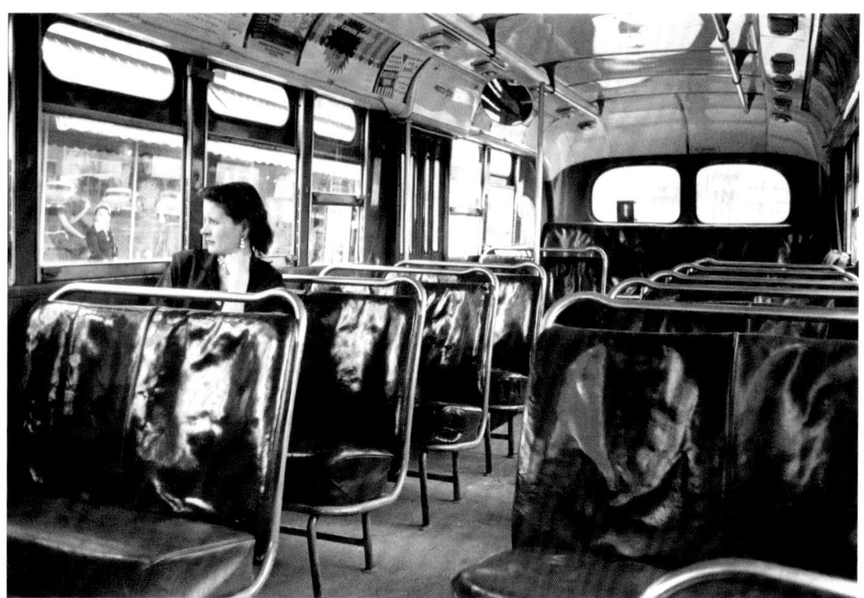

FIG. 26. Dan Weiner (American, 1919–1959). *Bus Boycott, Montgomery, Alabama*. 1956. Gelatin silver print, 6 5⁄8 x 9 5⁄8" (16.8 x 24.5 cm)

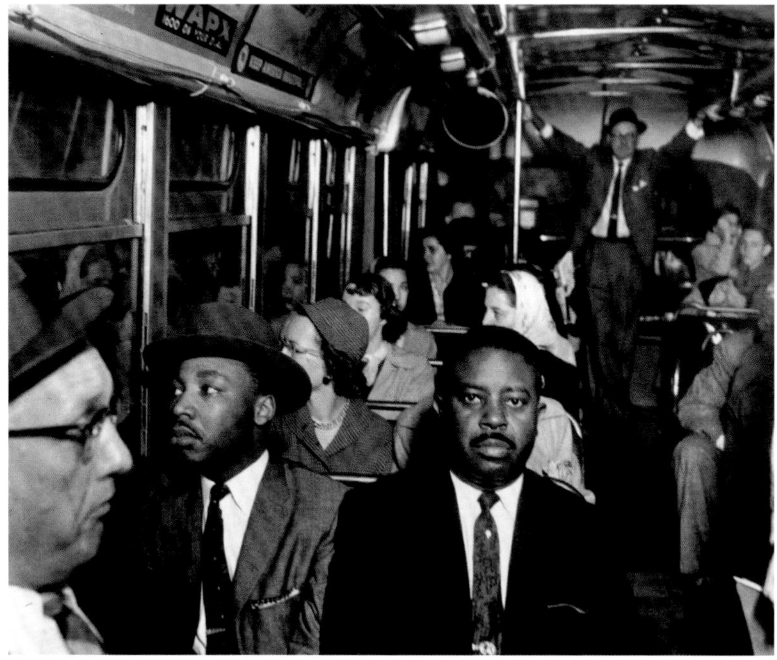

FIG. 27. Ernest C. Withers (American, 1922–2007). *Dr. Martin Luther King, Jr., and Reverend Ralph Abernathy on First Desegregated Bus, Montgomery, Alabama.* December 21, 1956. Gelatin silver print, 8 ¼ x 10 ¼" (21 x 26 cm). LIBRARY OF CONGRESS, PRINTS & PHOTOGRAPHS DIVISION

desegregated bus ride in Montgomery, on December 21, 1956, about a year after Rosa Parks refused to give up her seat **[FIG. 27]**.

In New Orleans, streetcars remained segregated until May 30, 1958. After a decisive court order by Judge J. Skelly Wright, the race screens were removed and destroyed overnight and the holes in the backs of the seats filled in. Pictures like *Trolley*, then, in the words of curator Peter Galassi, "mark Frank's book with the stamp of another time."[41] When the image was circulated on the cover of *The Americans*, in 1960, the streetcars in New Orleans were no longer segregated.

In 1959 the photographer Lee Friedlander shot his own streetcar picture **[FIG. 28]**. Despite the similarities in composition, the images feel worlds apart. Friedlander's picture lacks the perfect frontality of Frank's, and, crucially, the public transportation it depicts was no longer segregated. Frank was an important influence on Friedlander and the latter knew of *Trolley* when he made his image, but, as he himself has remarked, "any photographer who hangs around New Orleans long enough would make a streetcar picture"—it is a ubiquitous New Orleans subject.[42] After leaving SNCC in the fall of 1964, Lyon briefly moved to New Orleans, where he, too, made a streetcar image **[FIG. 29]**. Like many other photographers, he was responding to the "enormous shadow of Robert," he said.[43]

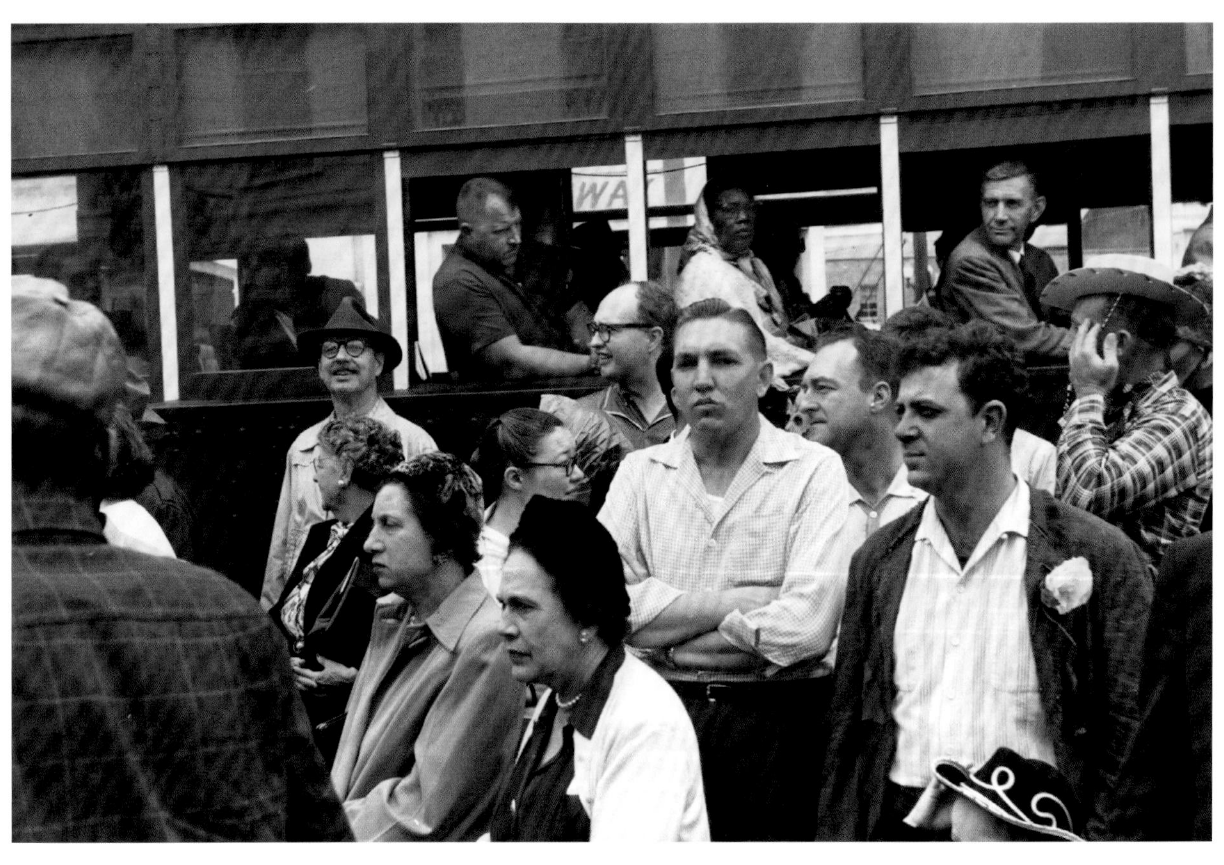

FIG. 28. Lee Friedlander (American, born 1934). *New Orleans, Louisiana*. 1959. Gelatin silver print, printed later, 8 ½ x 12 ¾" (21.6 x 32.4 cm). COURTESY FRAENKEL GALLERY, SAN FRANCISCO

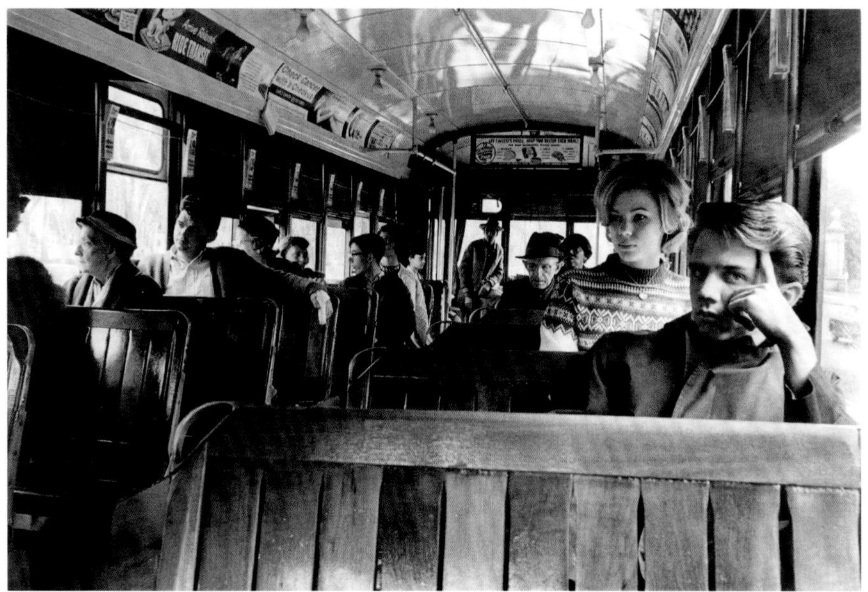

FIG. 29. Danny Lyon (American, born 1942). *Saint Charles Street Trolley, Louisiana*. 1964. Gelatin silver print, 9 × 13 ½" (22.8 × 34.2 cm). THE MUSEUM OF MODERN ART, NEW YORK. PURCHASE

Frank himself had been responding to the influence of other photographers, most notably Walker Evans. The structure of *The Americans* was indebted to Evans's 1938 *American Photographs*, a book of around the same size (with eighty-seven photographs to Frank's eighty-three).[44] Although they were then unpublished, it is very likely that Frank also knew Evans's extensive series of subway portraits, made with a hidden portable camera between 1938 and 1941, which captured the unguarded expressions of commuting passengers **[FIG. 30]**.[45] As a staff photographer and editor at *Fortune*, Evans was able to provide assignments for friends and photographers he admired. With Evans's encouragement, Frank was commissioned to photograph Pennsylvania Railroad's Congressional train, which ran between New York and Washington, D.C., and the images were published in *Fortune*'s November 1955 issue. Many of these pictures were made from the perspective of an outsider, observing the whispered conversations of powerful men **[FIG. 31]**. Ironically, the Arkansas State Police found a copy of this issue of *Fortune* in Frank's car on the night of his arrest, and Frank believed it may have provided enough proof of his legitimacy to lead to his release.[46]

—

Frank became a U.S. citizen in October 1963, five years after *The Americans* was first published and a year and a half after participating in a major two-person exhibition at The Museum of Modern Art. That 1962 show, shared with the

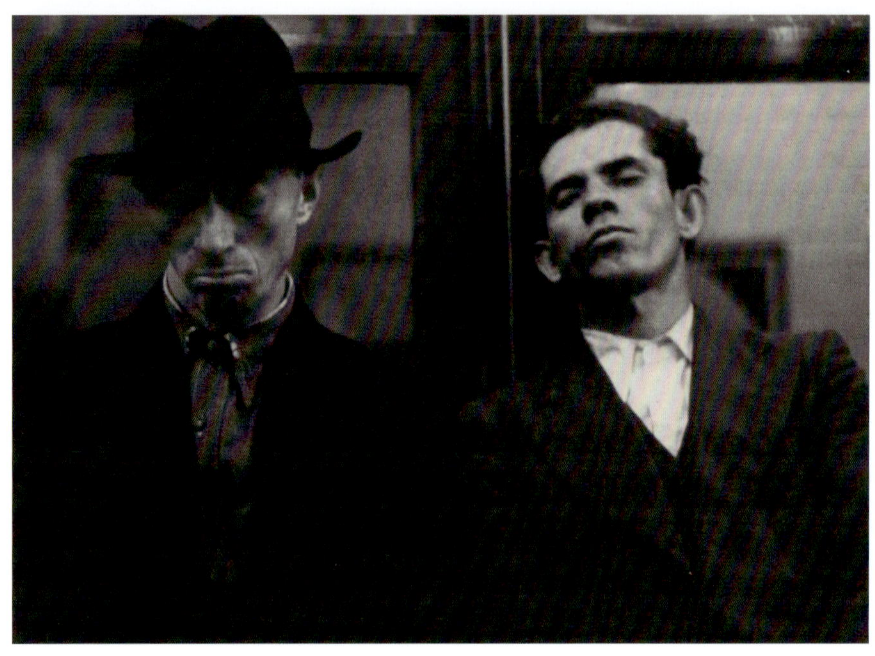

FIG. 30. Walker Evans (American, 1903–1975). *Subway Portrait*. 1938–41. Gelatin silver print, 3 ¾ × 5 ¼" (9.6 × 13.4 cm). THE MUSEUM OF MODERN ART, NEW YORK. PURCHASE

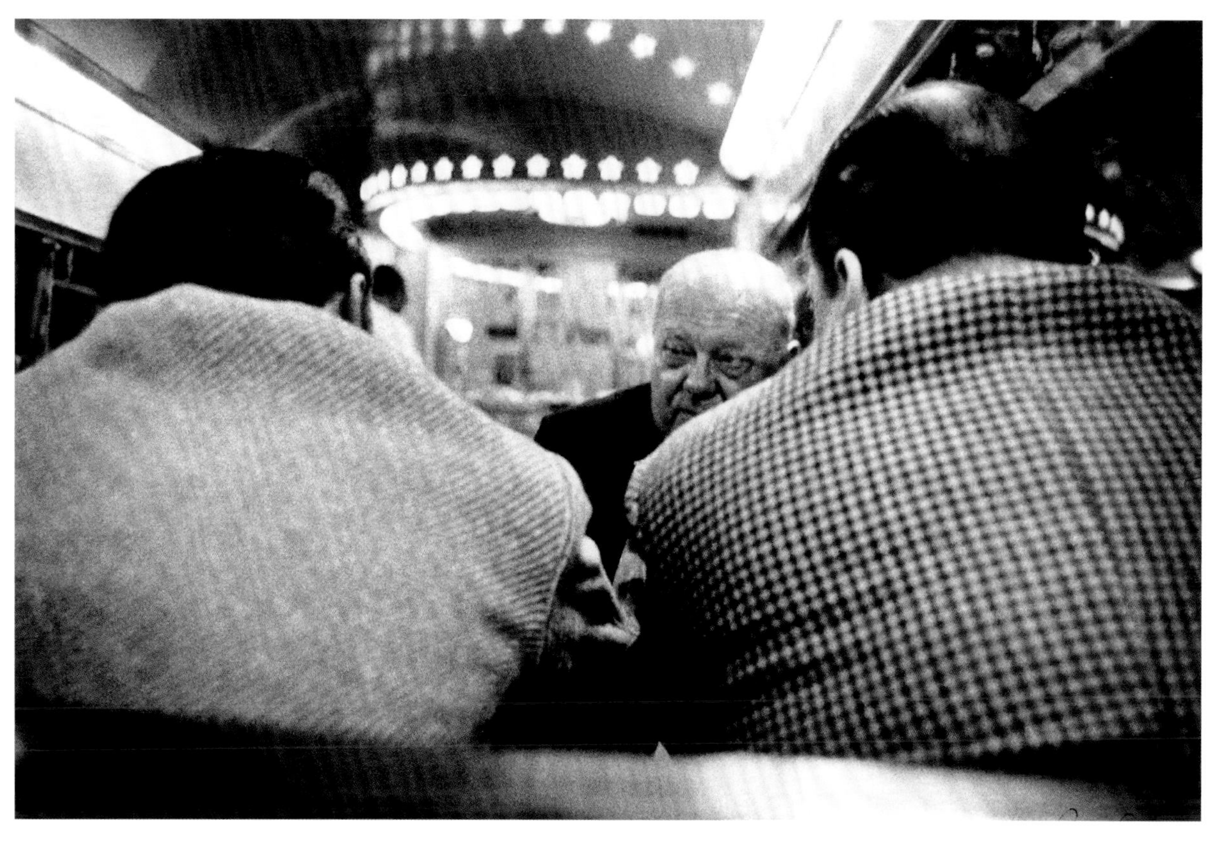

FIG. 31. Robert Frank (American, born Switzerland, 1924–2019). *En Route from New York to Washington, Club Car*. 1954 or 1955. Gelatin silver print, 10 15/16 x 13 7/8" (27.8 x 35.2 cm). THE MUSEUM OF FINE ARTS, HOUSTON. THE TARGET COLLECTION OF AMERICAN PHOTOGRAPHY, MUSEUM PURCHASE FUNDED BY TARGET STORES

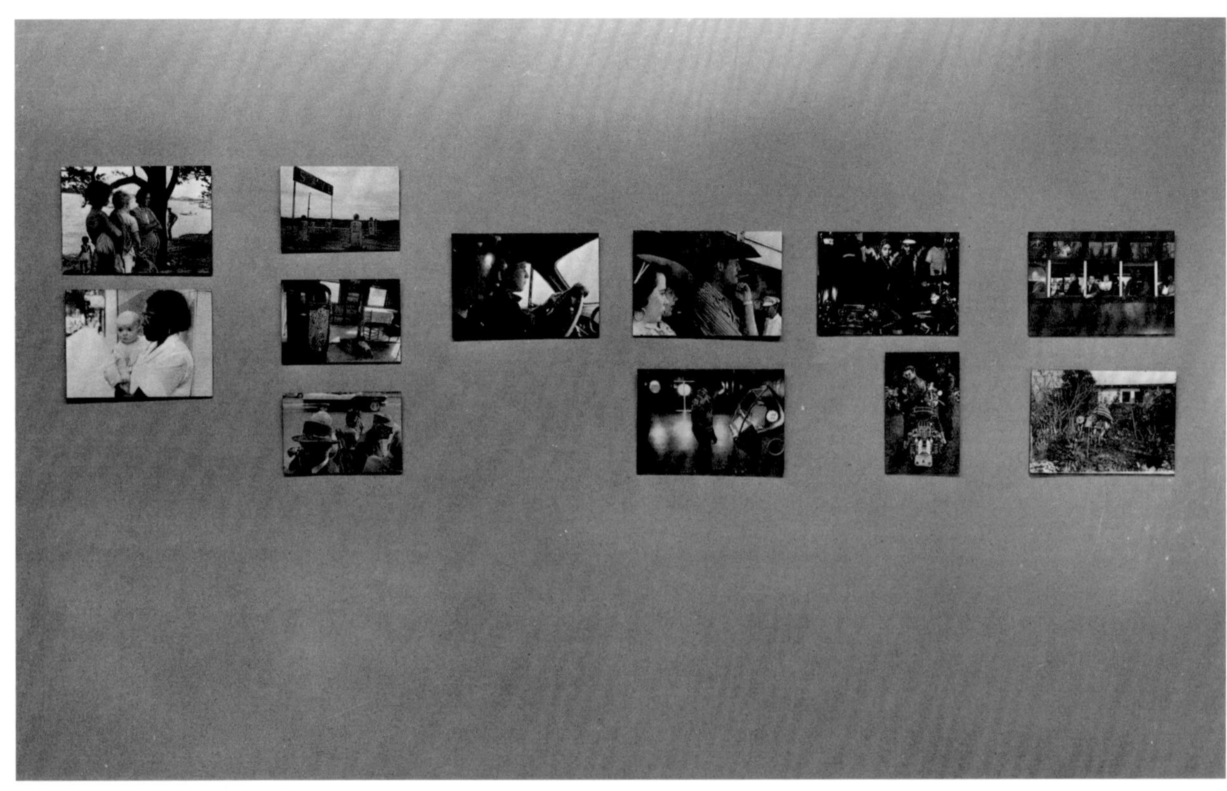

FIG. 32. Photographs from Frank's *The Americans* in the exhibition *Harry Callahan and Robert Frank*, with *Trolley—New Orleans* at upper right, The Museum of Modern Art, New York, January 30–April 1, 1962. Photo: Rolf Petersen. THE MUSEUM OF MODERN ART ARCHIVES, NEW YORK

photographer Harry Callahan, included many images from *The Americans*, including *Trolley* **[FIG. 32]**.[47] It also featured a newer body of work that Frank called From the Bus **[FIG. 33]**, made in the summer of 1958, before *The Americans* was published in the United States. Unlike that vast project, for From the Bus Frank worked within narrow parameters: all the pictures were taken from the window of a New York city bus as it made its way through Midtown Manhattan **[FIGS. 34, 35]**. For Frank, From the Bus marked a key shift between still photography and the moving and multipart images he would embrace for the rest of his career. "These photographs represent my last project in photography," he wrote in *The Lines of My Hand* in 1972. "When I selected the pictures and put them together I knew and I felt that I had come to the end of a chapter. And in it was the beginning of something new."[48]

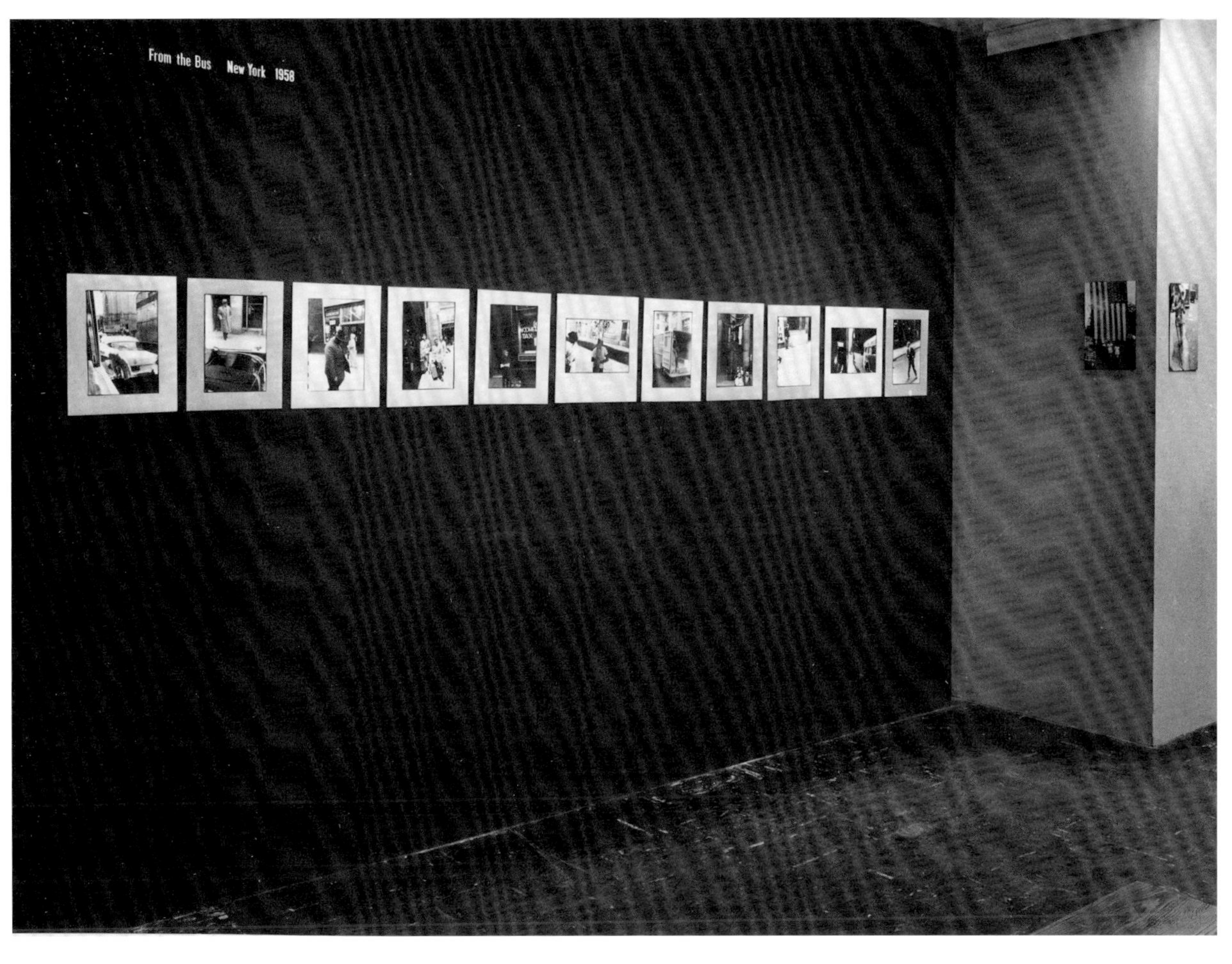

FIG. 33. Frank's series From the Bus in the exhibition *Harry Callahan and Robert Frank*, The Museum of Modern Art, New York, January 30–April 1, 1962. Photo: Rolf Petersen. THE MUSEUM OF MODERN ART ARCHIVES, NEW YORK

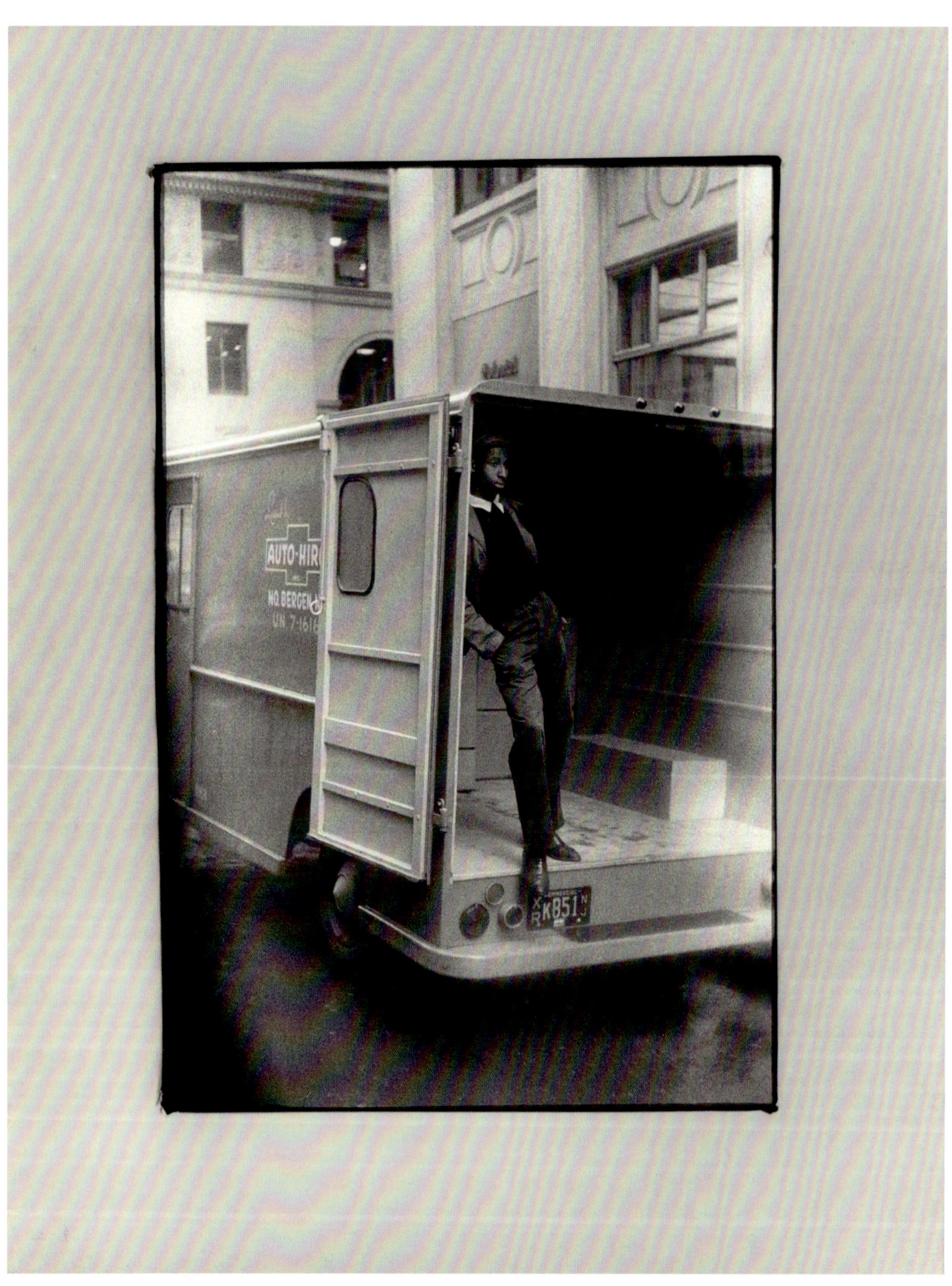
AUTO-HIR
NO. BERGEN
UN 7-1616
KB51

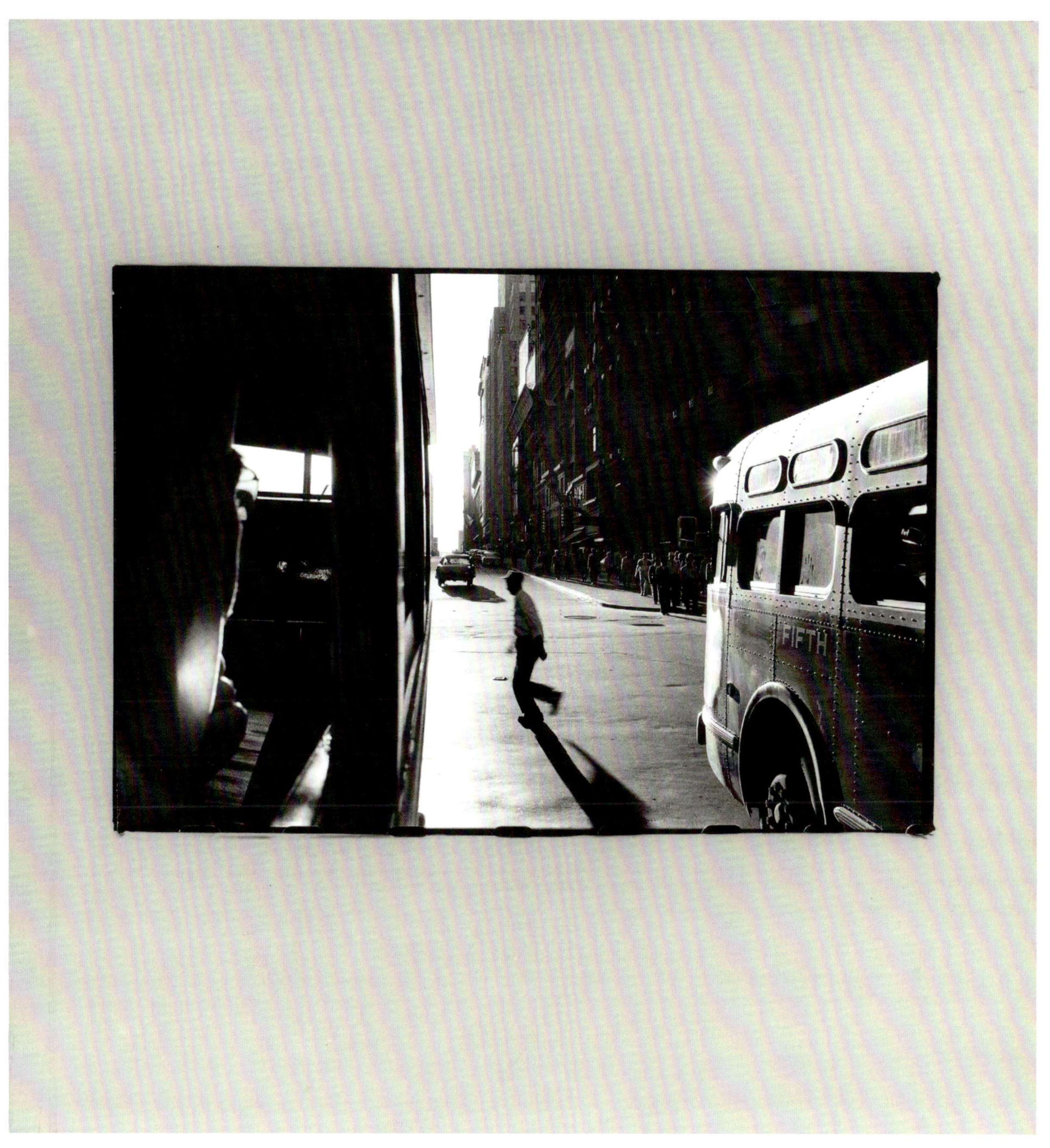

FIGS. 34, 35. Robert Frank (American, born Switzerland, 1924–2019). Photographs from the series From the Bus, 1958. Gelatin silver prints mounted on fiberboard, opposite: 13 7/8 x 10 11/16" (35.2 x 27.2 cm); above: 13 15/16 x 13 1/4" (35.4 x 33.7 cm). THE NATIONAL GALLERY OF ART, WASHINGTON, D.C. ROBERT FRANK COLLECTION, ROBERT B. MENSCHEL FUND

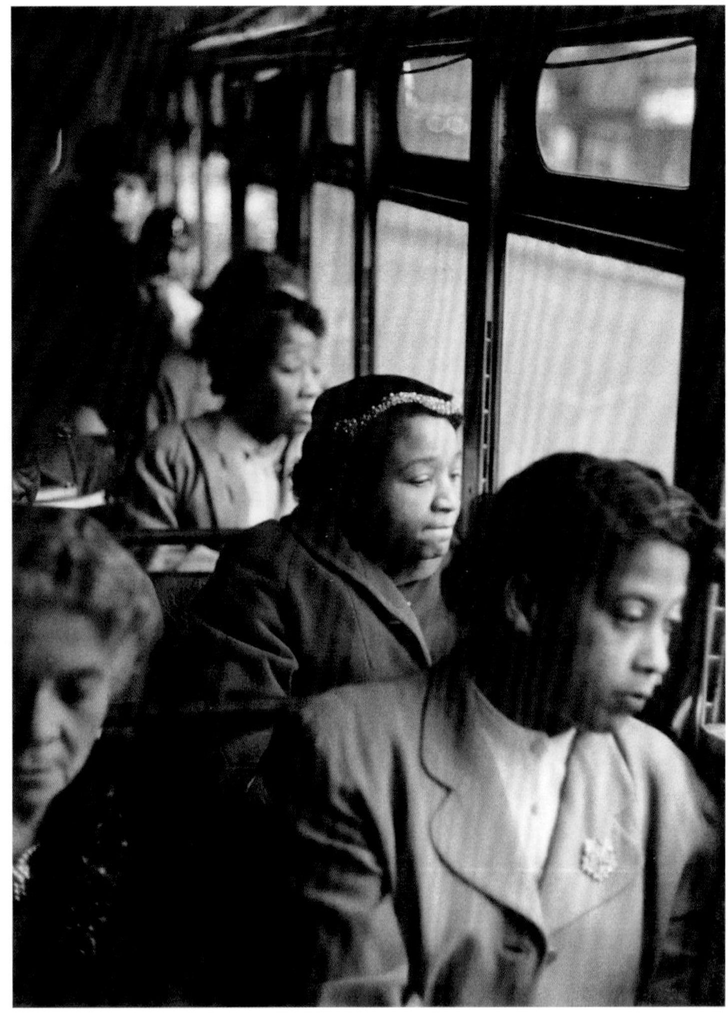

FIG. 36. Roy DeCarava (American, 1919–2009). *Women, uptown bus.* 1948. Gelatin silver print, 14 x 11" (35.6 x 27.9 cm)

Frank was living in New York when he made From the Bus, and the series follows in a long tradition of images chronicling the role public transportation has played in the daily lives of the city's denizens, including, for example, a photograph by Roy DeCarava, made in New York a decade earlier, in which three women riding an uptown bus tilt their heads at almost identical angles as they gaze out adjacent windows at the street below **[FIG. 36]**. Frank had photographed the interior of a New York city bus during his Guggenheim years **[FIG. 37]**, but in From the Bus he, too, was looking out at the world. "The Bus carries me thru

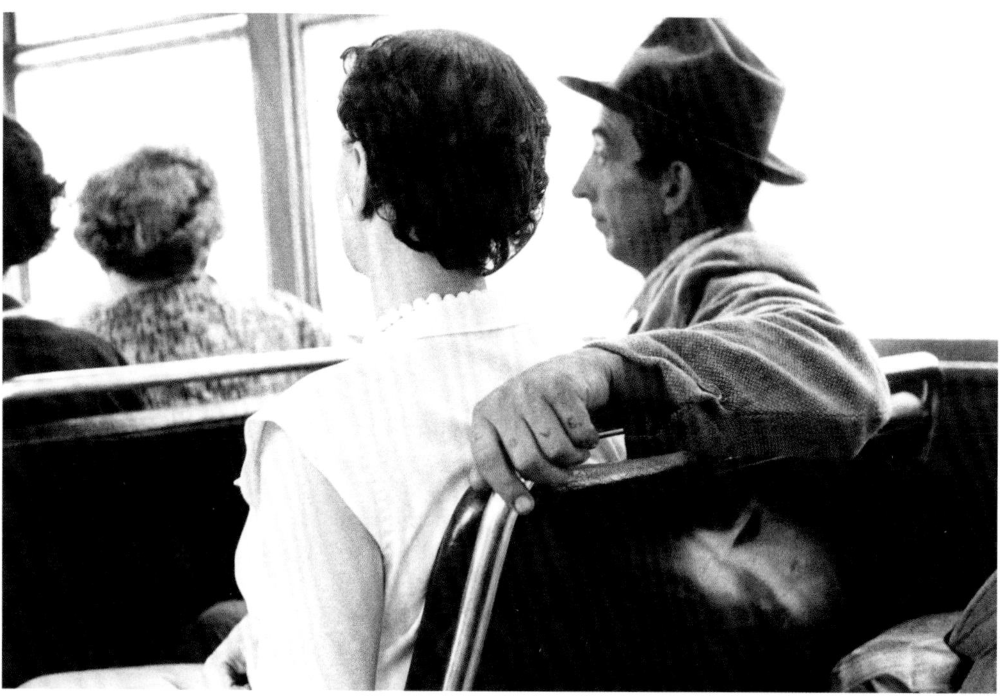

FIG. 37. Robert Frank (American, born Switzerland. 1924–2019). *New York City*. 1956. Gelatin silver print, printed 1970s, 8 ⅝ × 13 ⅛" (21.9 × 33.3 cm). THE MUSEUM OF MODERN ART, NEW YORK. GIFT OF SUSAN AND PETER MACGILL IN HONOR OF PETER GALASSI

the City," he wrote of his process. "I look out the window, I look at the people on the street, the Sun and the Traffic Lights. It has to do with desperation and endurance—I have always felt that about living in New York. Compassion and probably some understanding for New York's Concrete and its people."[49]

This sentiment is strikingly similar to Frank's description of the emotion he felt while making *The Americans*: "I think that at that time I was compassionate. I had compassion for the people on the street. That was the main meat of the book—that gave me the push—that made me work so hard until I knew I had something but I didn't even know I had America."[50] From the Bus and *Trolley* were made in very different cities and from very different vantages, but their connections accentuate the enduring significance of *Trolley*. Like the From the Bus pictures, *Trolley* is simply a street photograph made on a typical day in the United States: its implications about American society are conveyed through an image of everyday injustice rather than an instance of spectacular violence. Though New Orleans streetcars have long been desegregated, the photograph remains a powerful illumination of this country's enduring racism and inequality.

NOTES

1. Robert Frank to his parents, winter 1955, reprinted in Anne Wilkes Tucker and Philip Brookman, eds., *Robert Frank: New York to Nova Scotia*, exh. cat. (Houston: Museum of Fine Arts, 1986), p. 28. The Tucker and Brookman book reprints numerous primary documents in full. Many of these are also reproduced in Sarah Greenough, ed., *Looking In: Robert Frank's "The Americans,"* exh. cat. (Washington, D.C.: National Gallery of Art; Göttingen: Steidl, 2009).

2. *Canal Street—New Orleans* [fig. 2] was also included in Frank's book *The Americans* (New York: Grove, 1959), where it appears on the spread after *Trolley—New Orleans*. The volume is not paginated.

3. Frank, quoted in William S. Johnson, "Public Statements/Private Views: Shifting the Ground in the 1950s," in David Featherstone, ed., *Observations: Essays on Documentary Photography* (Carmel, Calif.: Friends of Photography, 1984), p. 90.

4. Danny Lyon, conversation with the author, March 5, 2020.

5. Frank's 1954 Guggenheim Fellowship application is reprinted in Tucker and Brookman, *New York to Nova Scotia*, p. 20.

6. Frank, quoted in Dennis Wheeler, "Robert Frank Interviewed," *Criteria* 3, no. 2 (June 1977): 7.

7. Jack Kerouac, introduction to Frank, *The Americans*. The descriptor was also used, a few years earlier, in the title of an article in *U.S. Camera*: Byron Dobell, "Featured Pictures: Robert Frank—The Photographer as Poet," *U.S. Camera* 17, no. 9 (September 1954): 77–84.

8. Frank, "A Statement . . . ," in Tom Maloney, ed., *1958 U.S. Camera Annual* (New York: U.S. Camera, 1957), p. 115.

9. Sid Kaplan made this remark in a group meeting about *Trolley—New Orleans* in the Department of Photography at The Museum of Modern Art, October 10, 2013. See transcription in report compiled by Sarah Montross, January 27, 2015, Department of Photography, MoMA.

10. This was Frank's second arrest while on the road photographing for *The Americans*. The first was in Detroit, in July, after police found him in possession of two license plates (his own and the expired plate that had belonged to the previous owner of his car).

11. R. E. Brown, Lieutenant, Arkansas State Police, to Alan R. Templeton, Captain, Criminal Investigation Division, Arkansas State Police, December 19, 1955, reprinted in Tucker and Brookman, *New York to Nova Scotia*, p. 24.

12. Frank to Walker Evans, November 9, 1955, reprinted in ibid., pp. 25–26.

13. Frank, "Comments at Wellesley," in Eugenia Parry Janis and Wendy MacNeil, eds., *Photography within the Humanities* (Danbury, N.H.: Addison House, 1977), p. 56.

14. Frank was not a U.S. citizen at the time of his Guggenheim Fellowship application, but he had lived in the United States for more than eight years and had been married to a U.S. citizen for more than four.

15. Frank, quoted in Nicholas Dawidoff, "The Man Who Saw America," *New York Times Magazine*, July 2, 2015.

16. See Sarah Gordon and Paul Roth, "Map and Chronology," in Greenough, *Looking In*, p. 365. Gordon and Roth's chronology is an exhaustive account of Frank's career before and after *The Americans*.

17. Ibid. Leica would use photographs by Frank in its advertisements from 1954 to 1956, the years he was photographing across the United States (p. 367).

18. Steichen also served as a juror for many prizes Frank won in the early 1950s. In 1952 Frank produced three copies of his hand-bound book *Black White and Things*, which includes photographs he made in Europe, South America, and the United States. He kept one copy for himself and one for his father and sent the third to Steichen. The book remains in MoMA's collection.

19. For an in-depth comparison of the two projects, see Eric J. Sandeen, "Edward Steichen, Robert Frank, and American Modernism," in *Picturing an Exhibition: The Family of Man and 1950s America* (Albuquerque: University of New Mexico Press, 1995), pp. 155–81.

20. Evans, "Robert Frank," in Maloney, *1958 U.S. Camera Annual*, p. 90.

21. Frank, quoted in Philip Gefter, "Snapshots from the American Road," *New York Times*, December 12, 2008.

22. Ibid. Frank continued to view *Trolley—New Orleans* through a personal lens. In one of his most personal films, *Conversations in Vermont* (1969)—about which he narrated, "It's about the past and the present, some kind of a family album"—a print of *Trolley* is pictured amid stacks of family photographs.

23. In his Guggenheim Fellowship application Frank listed two possible publishers for his project, both European: "1) M. Delpire of 'NEUF', Paris, for book form. 2) Mr. Kubler of 'DU' [Zurich] for an entire issue of his magazine."
24. Henri Cartier-Bresson, *The Europeans* (New York: Simon Schuster, 1955). See Greenough, "Disordering the Senses: Guggenheim Fellowship," in *Looking In*, p. 135.
25. Frank to Barney Rosset, April 22, 1959, reproduced in Greenough, *Looking In*, p. 359.
26. Frank in "An Evening with Robert Frank," a public conversation between the photographer and the curators Jeff L. Rosenheim and Sarah Greenough at the Metropolitan Museum of Art, New York, October 9, 2009. A recording of the conversation was released as an episode of the podcast series *Photographs—Special Exhibitions*, produced by the Metropolitan Museum of Art.
27. The book's copyright date is 1959. Gordon and Roth note that it was published in late fall 1959 and "officially released" by Grove Press on January 15, 1960. See "Map and Chronology," p. 368.
28. *Popular Photography* 46, no. 5 (May 1960): 104–6.
29. Ibid.
30. Frank, quoted in *Documentary Photography* (New York: Time-Life Books, 1972), p. 171.
31. Maurice Berger, "Robert Frank, Telling It Like It Was," *Lens* (blog), *New York Times*, January 15, 2015.
32. R. J. Smith, *American Witness: The Art and Life of Robert Frank* (New York: Da Capo, 2017), p. 286n6.
33. Greenough, "Disordering the Senses: Guggenheim Fellowship," p. 122.
34. Elliott Erwitt, quoted in Dawidoff, "The Man Who Saw America."
35. Martin A. Berger, "The Formulas of Documentary Photography," in *Seeing through Race: A Reinterpretation of Civil Rights Photography* (Berkeley: University of California Press, 2011), p. 52.
36. However, as lawyer and social justice activist Bryan Stevenson has noted, violence is implicit even in "everyday" images of segregation: "Terrorism, the violence of lynching, is critical for understanding how you could have decades of Jim Crow. No one would have accepted drinking out of the inferior water fountain or going into the less desirable 'colored' bathroom unless violence could be exercised against you for noncompliance with segregation with impunity." Stevenson in conversation with Sarah Lewis, "Truth & Reconciliation: Images, Narrative, and Racial Justice," *Aperture*, no. 230 (Spring 2018): 27.
37. Lorraine Hansberry, *The Movement: Documentary of a Struggle for Equality* (New York: Simon & Schuster, 1964), p. 26.
38. Ibid, p. 36.
39. Elizabeth Mullener, "Civil Rights Movement: Leaders on Both Sides Smoothed Way to Integration," *Times-Picayune* (New Orleans), June 16, 1993.
40. Jacob Lawrence, interview with Jackson Frost, April 2000, Phillips Collection Archives, Washington, D.C.
41. Peter Galassi, *Robert Frank in America*, exh. cat. (Göttingen: Steidl, 2014), p. 27.
42. Friedlander, conversation with the author, March 2, 2020. Friedlander had acquired a copy of *Les Américains* in 1958. See Galassi, *Friedlander*, exh. cat. (New York: The Museum of Modern Art, 2004), p. 33. As Greenough has noted, Frank's contact sheets from his Guggenheim-funded trips reveal a fixation on iconic subjects that might be considered representative of each city—such as hotels in Miami and streetcars and buses in New Orleans. See Greenough, "Disordering the Senses: Guggenheim Fellowship," p. 124.
43. Lyon, conversation with the author. Lyon would become very close with Frank, even moving in with him for a few months, but the two did not meet until 1967. See Lyon, "When Fathers Die: Remembering Robert Frank," *NYR Daily* (blog), *New York Review of Books*, September 27, 2019.
44. For a comparison of the two books, see Tod Papageorge, *Walker Evans and Robert Frank: An Essay on Influence* (New Haven, Conn.: Yale University Art Gallery, 1981).
45. Evans's subway portraits were not published as a photo-book until years later, in the volume *Many Are Called* (Boston: Houghton Mifflin, 1966).
46. Frank to Evans, November 9, 1955.
47. The exhibition was originally planned as a three-person show, with W. Eugene Smith, but Smith declined to participate.
48. Frank, *The Lines of My Hand* (New York: Lustrum, 1972), n.p.
49. Frank to Philip Brookman, December 27, 1977, quoted in Brookman, "The Silence of Recognition: Exhibiting Robert Frank's The Americans," in Greenough, *Looking In*, p. 326.
50. Frank, quoted in Wheeler, "Robert Frank Interviewed," p. 7.

FOR FURTHER READING

Brookman, Philip, and Vicente Todolí. *Robert Frank: Storylines*. Exh. cat. London: Tate, 2004.

Dawidoff, Nicholas. "The Man Who Saw America." *New York Times Magazine*, July 2, 2015.

Eskildsen, Ute, ed. *Robert Frank: Hold Still—Keep Going*. Exh. cat. Zurich: Scalo, 2001.

Galassi, Peter. *Robert Frank in America*. Exh. cat. Göttingen: Steidl, 2014.

Greenough, Sarah, ed. *Looking In: Robert Frank's "The Americans."* Exh. cat. Washington, D.C.: National Gallery of Art; Göttingen: Steidl, 2009.

Greenough, Sarah, and Philip Brookman. *Robert Frank: Moving Out*. Exh. cat. Washington, D.C.: National Gallery of Art, 1994.

Smith, R. J. *American Witness: The Art and Life of Robert Frank*. New York: Da Capo, 2017.

Tucker, Anne Wilkes, and Philip Brookman, eds. *Robert Frank: New York to Nova Scotia*. Exh. cat. Houston: Museum of Fine Arts, 1986.

BY ROBERT FRANK

The Americans. Introduction by Jack Kerouac. Göttingen: Steidl, 2017. First published in 1959 by Grove (New York).

The Lines of My Hand. Göttingen: Steidl, 2017. First published in 1972 by Lustrum (New York).

ALSO OF INTEREST

Israel, Laura, dir. *Don't Blink—Robert Frank*. 2015. USA. Grasshopper Film. 82 min.

Produced by the Department of Publications
The Museum of Modern Art, New York

Edited by Rebecca Roberts
Series designed by Miko McGinty and Rita Jules
Layout by Amanda Washburn
Production by Matthew Pimm
Proofread by Naomi Falk
Printed and bound by Ofset Yapimevi, Istanbul

Typeset in Ideal Sans
Printed on 150 gsm Magno Satin

Published by The Museum of Modern Art
11 West 53 Street
New York, NY 10019-5497
www.moma.org

ISBN: 978-1-63345-119-3

Distributed in the United States and Canada by
ARTBOOK | D.A.P.
75 Broad Street
Suite 630
New York, NY 10004
www.artbook.com

Distributed outside the United States and Canada by
Thames & Hudson Ltd
181A High Holborn
London WC1V 7QX
www.thamesandhudson.com

Printed and bound in Turkey

PHOTOGRAPH CREDITS

TRUSTEES OF THE MUSEUM OF MODERN ART